In Some Intrinsic Way
Everything Bends Toward Infinity
Visible Descants & Public Displays

Billboard Art by

Andrew Franck

ISBN-13: 978-1523943005

ISBN-10: 1523943009

CONTENTS

Whether addressing a specific audience or the general public, billboards and displays are largely in the service of announcing or selling. Along roadsides, in store windows, on various screens and throughout the Internet, they promote product availability, a brand, a service, an opportunity. In a nutshell, they *advertise*, a word whose origin comes from the Latin *ad vertere* meaning "to turn toward." Advertising draws, beckons, conveys, getting the viewer to turn toward and, depending on the draw, tune in their attention. A great deal of signage seeks to generate increased consumption, or portray an enterprise's attractiveness, viability and success. Conspicuous surfaces on a sizable scale are leased out to corporate sales, to special interest groups, political candidates, religious organizations and government agencies. A few of these function in the role of public service announcements, intending to influence better sense and good judgment. All in all, wide-scale attention-getting media seeks to sway by reason, or appeal to emotion. At times the content is worth telling. Sometimes not. Apart from a small serving of conceptual art in galleries and museums, little of what yearns to be said concerning the metaphysical, the imaginative, the ponderable is openly available in a significant textual form. Nonetheless, the following aphorisms, mottos and mantras promote an on-the-spot context for the observer to reflect, consider and wonder. Through hints and proposition, they visibly urge culture to occupy itself, consider its nature, its disposition, nadirs and peaks, account for its own narratives, grasp its character, and summon its worth for the future. Among other things.

Appreciatively, a number of these descants seemed to arrive blown in by something akin to an unexplainable current of air. Others came to be through observation, musings, feelings of outrage, or through a rush of sheer irony. Overall, they aim to serve as focused articulations, nurturing an ongoing dynamism with regard to ideas, opinion and action. Though meant to be exhibited much like large-scale advertising, a number of small-scale presentations have made their way onto walls and ceilings using stencils and paint. Other media were employed in a few instances including decorative lighting, colored sand, broken glass, Chinese bowls, assorted miniature toys and bird feathers. Given opportune circumstances, an assortment of these have been displayed in park settings, near government monuments, sporting events and shopping malls. Clearly, there are many more contexts and possibilities given the overabundance of public advertising space and a dearth of inspired market-led concern. Here, assembled in book form (though regrettably not in their original lively colors), these billboards collectively motion to the observer: feel invited, be stirred, bend this moment a little closer toward infinity.

AF

3 dimensions>

darknessspacematter

2 dimensions>

color

1 dimension>

light

1

belief

is a

four

letter

word

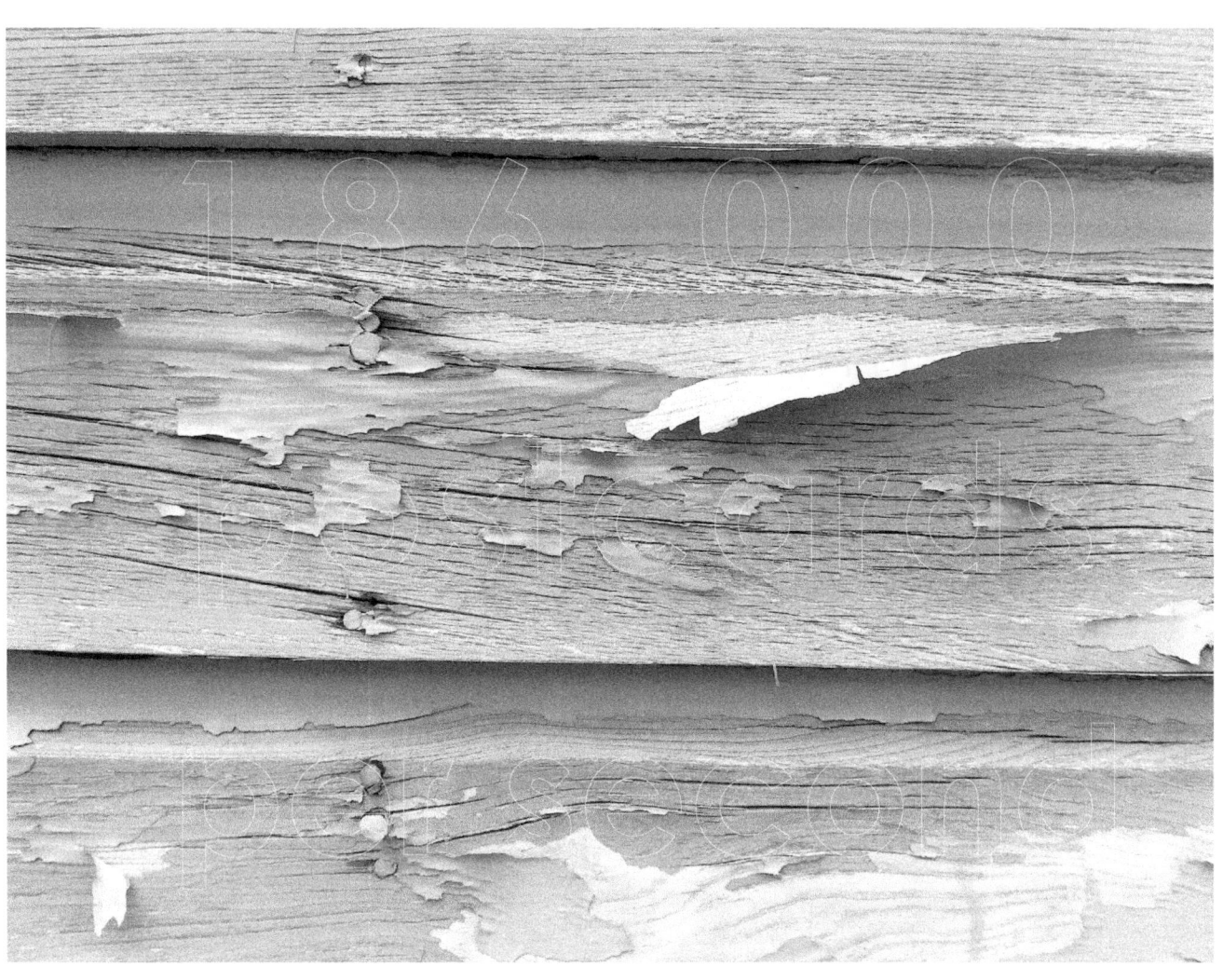

a challenge

for the modern soul

is to lift information into

streaming forces of warmth

a
darkness
backlit by
black

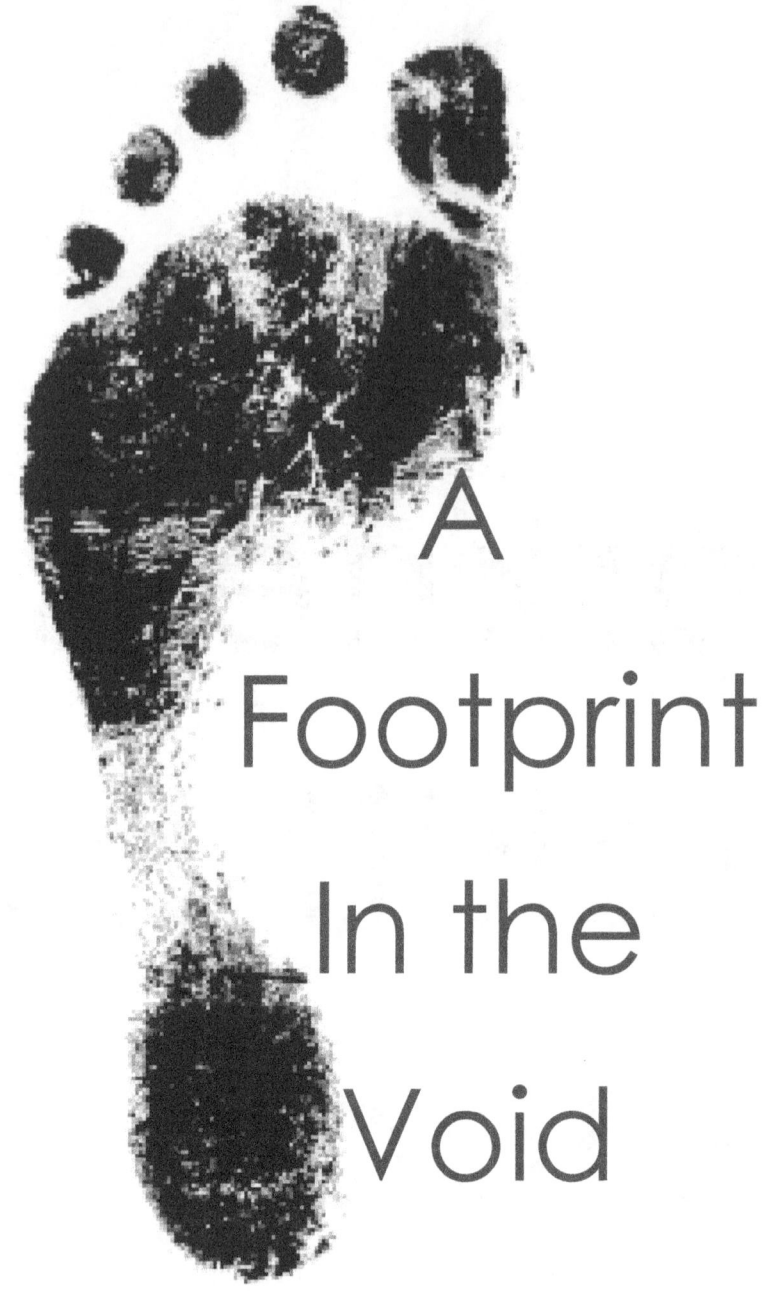

A

Footprint

In the

Void

a little
embryology
goes a long
way

a split second
to feel the
spatial
dynamics

a world of assembled broken assemblages

accept the body's

extinction

with love

accessing the
Unheard,
SOMETHING
erases sound

Disturbingly, the force of conviction can render you immortal

all words

as a

whisper

thru your

body

altogether, let's eavesdrop on the after-sound

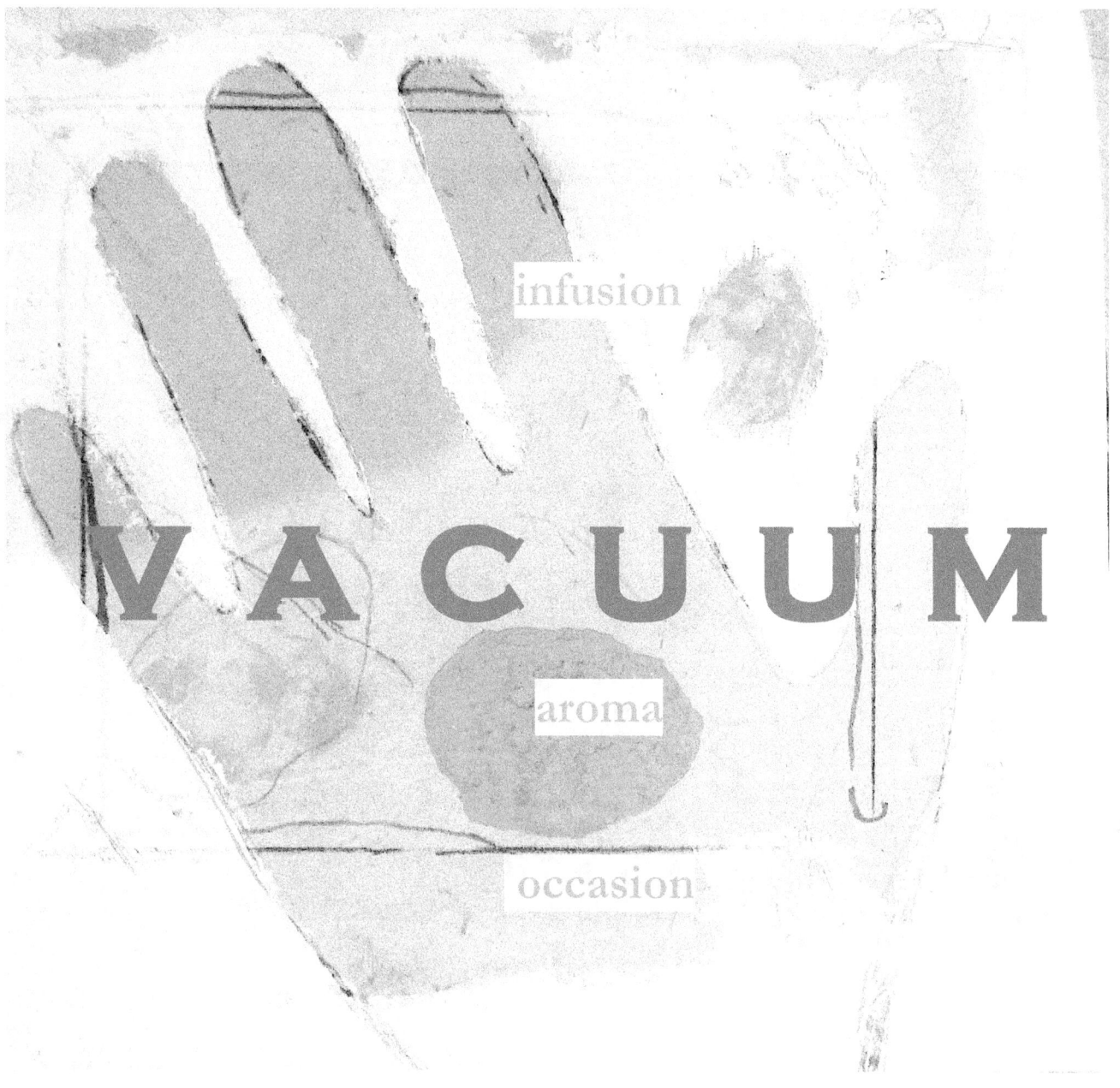

infusion

VACUUM

aroma

occasion

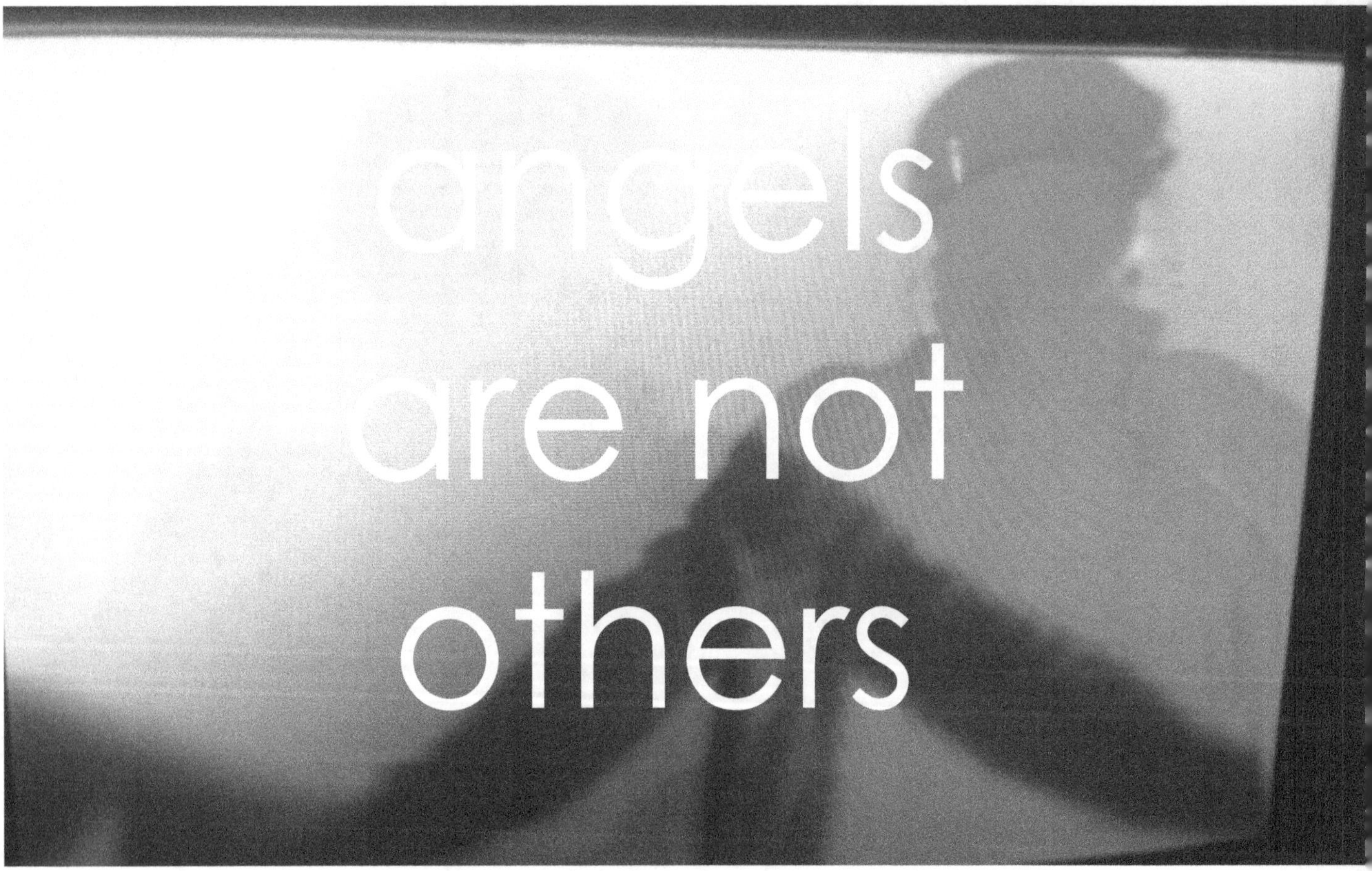
angels
are not
others

apparitions
are this
ghost
country

appearances invite us
no matter what

Are you seeking that special someone who'll make a great effort to deeply misunderstand you?

♈

a splendid
image of self

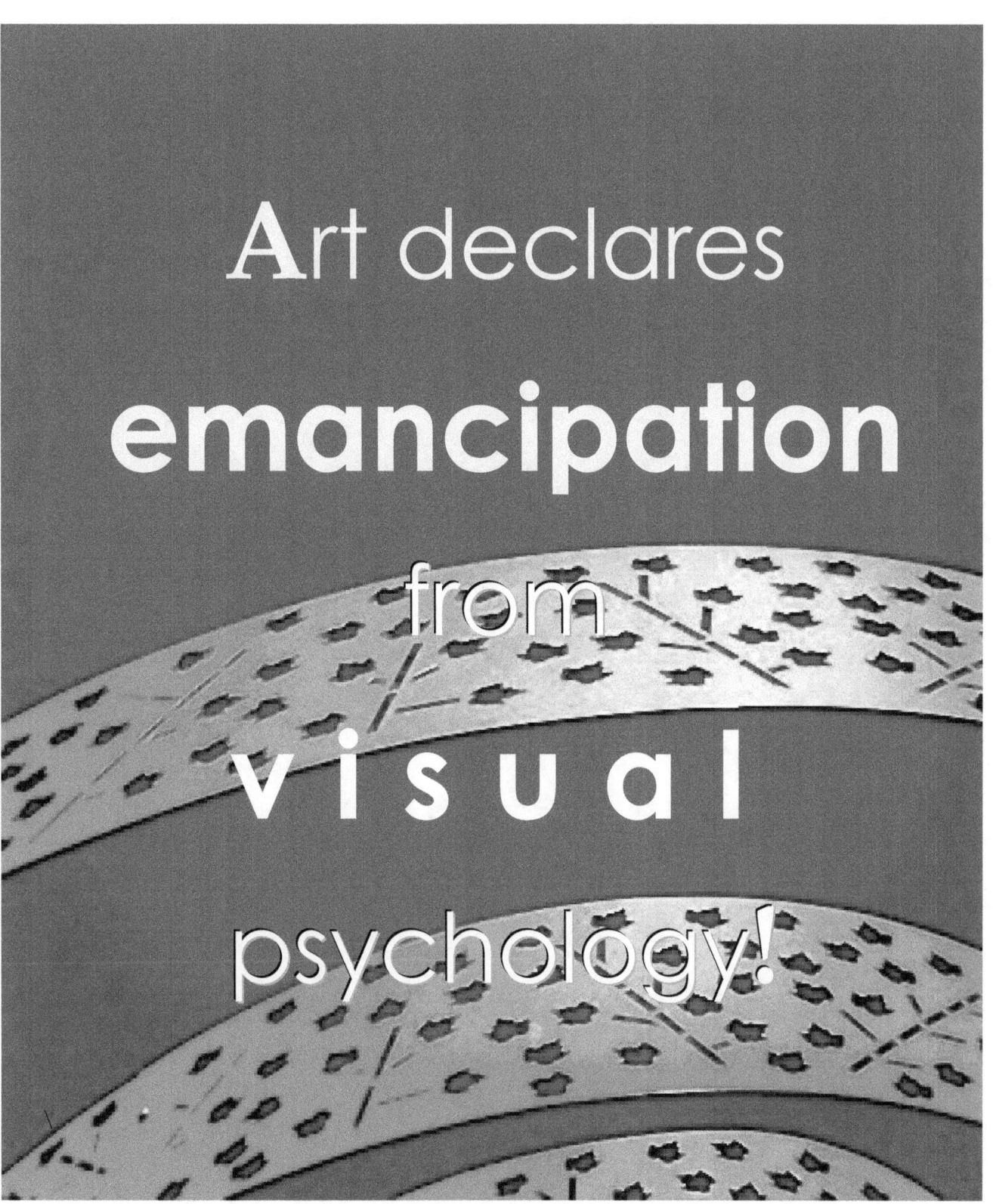

Art declares

emancipation

from

v i s u a l

psychology!

AS ABOVE ∞

INSIDE ∞

∞OUT

∞BELOW

incoming soul
spring-in
offspring
incarnated soul

a s i a :

three-thousand
neat-ankled
daughters
dispersed
far and wide

aspire to

forgive

the future

astral fresh joy

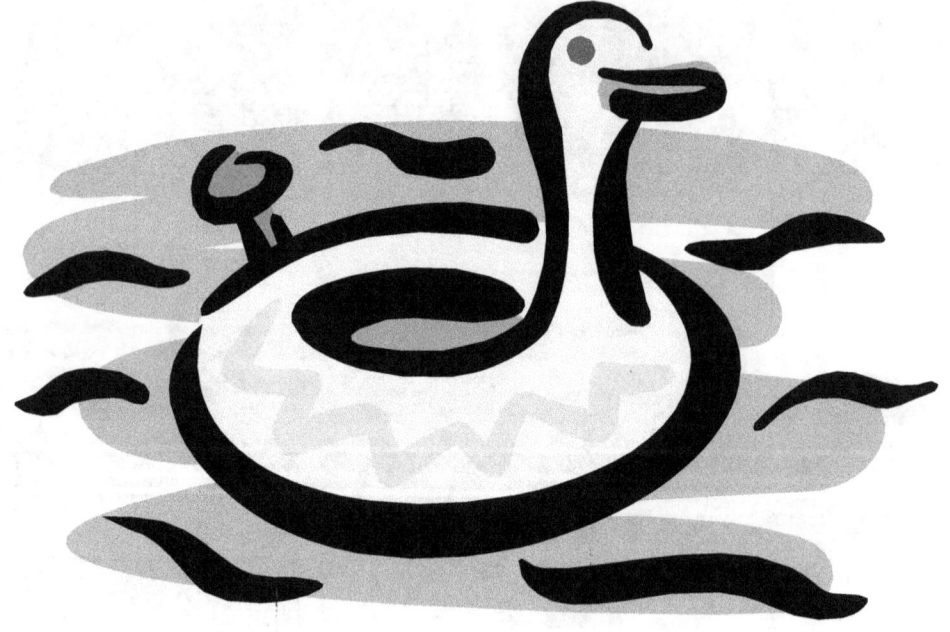

attention all beings

attention all beings:
attention all beings:

attention **all** beings

attention all beings:
attention all **beings**:

27

auditioning for life

?

avoid making spells

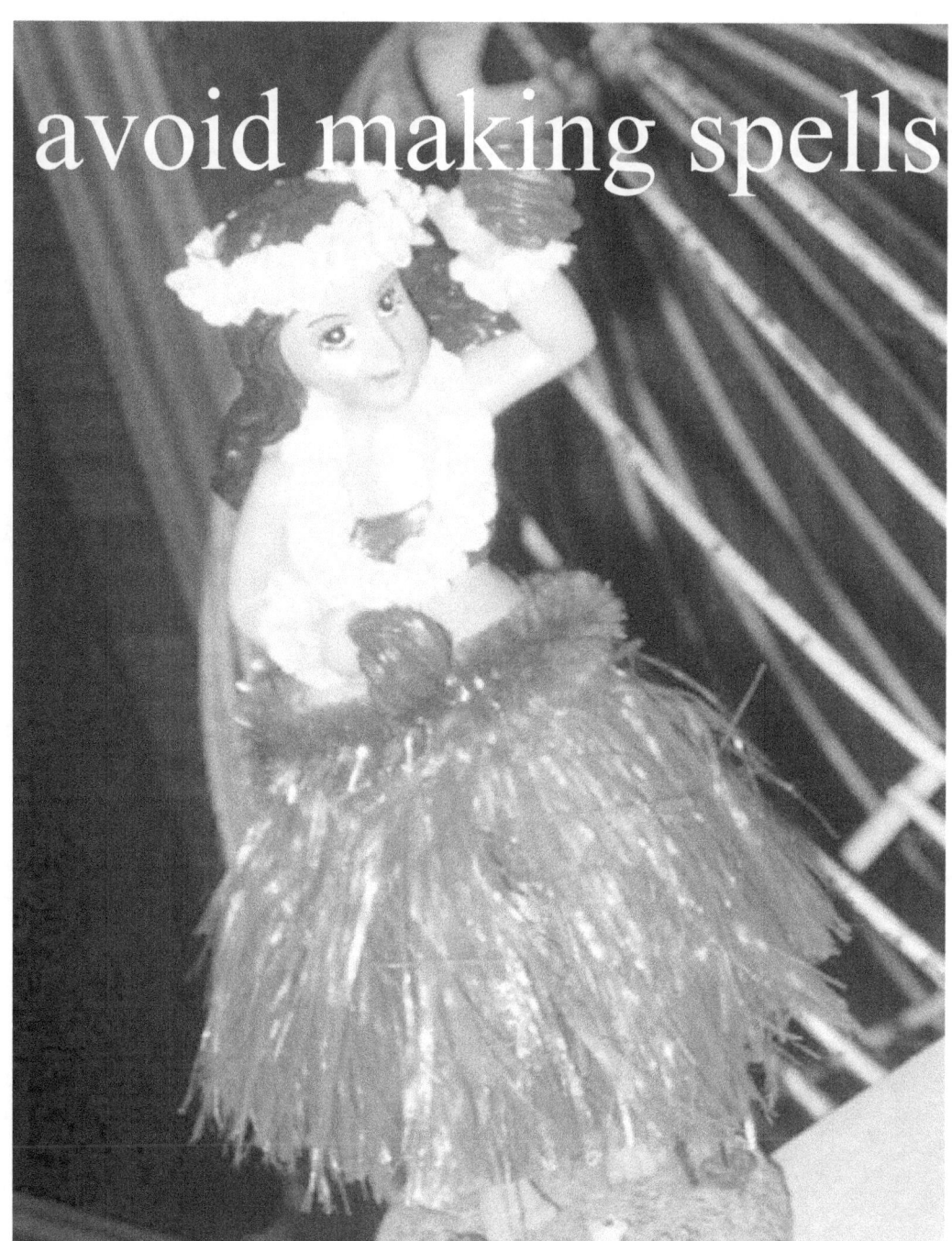

everlasting

conscience

motion

wisdom

hence, there's no need to believe in *anything*

awareness

is worth a

thousand

adventures

the sordid attitudes

of getting away with
as much as possible

&

applying oneself as
little as possible

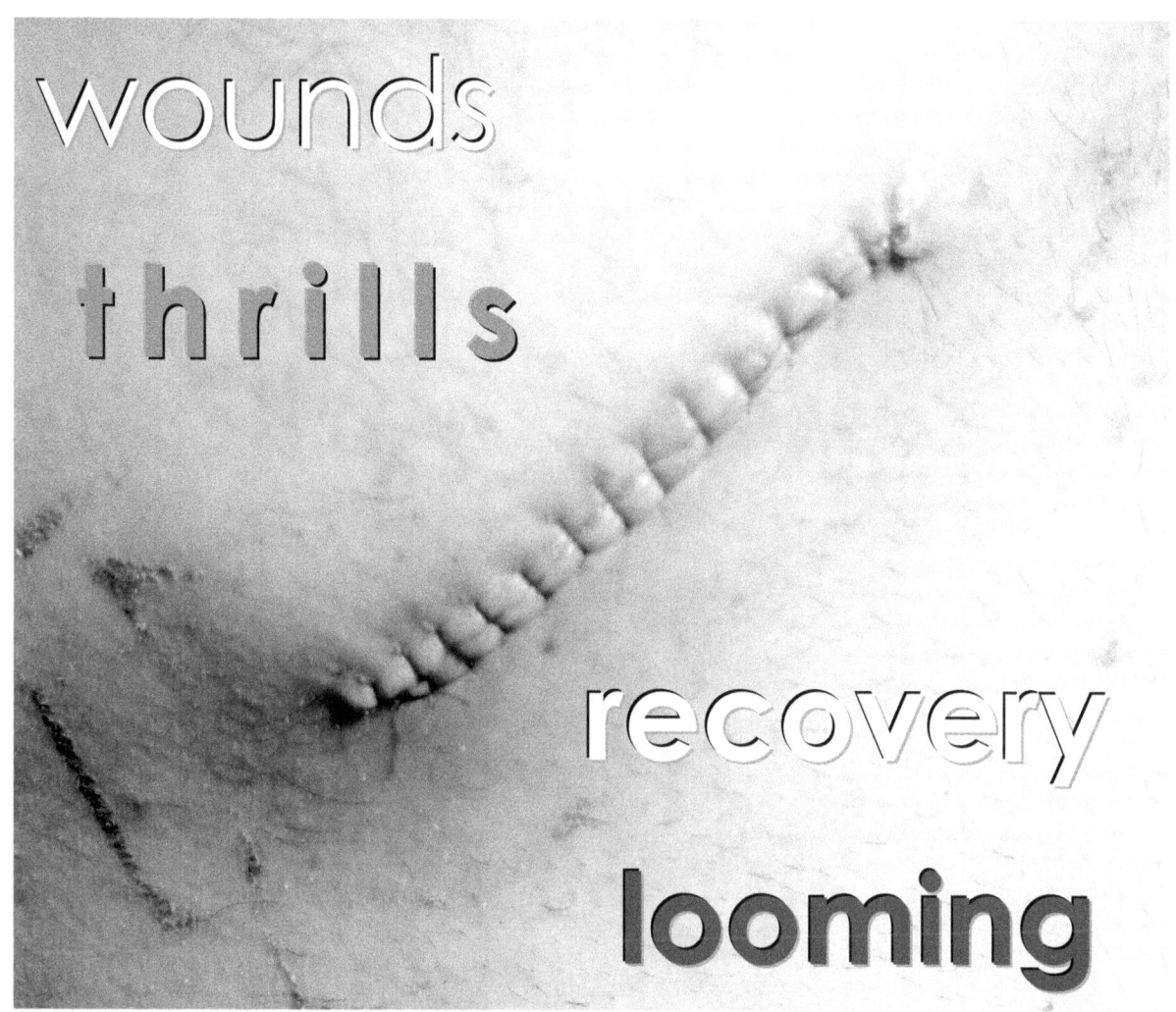

thrills

recovery

looming

be an
artist:
take the
unquestionably
cognitive
& make it
fuzzy

seeing there's
nowhere to
hide

be in all places
at once

beautiful

TO

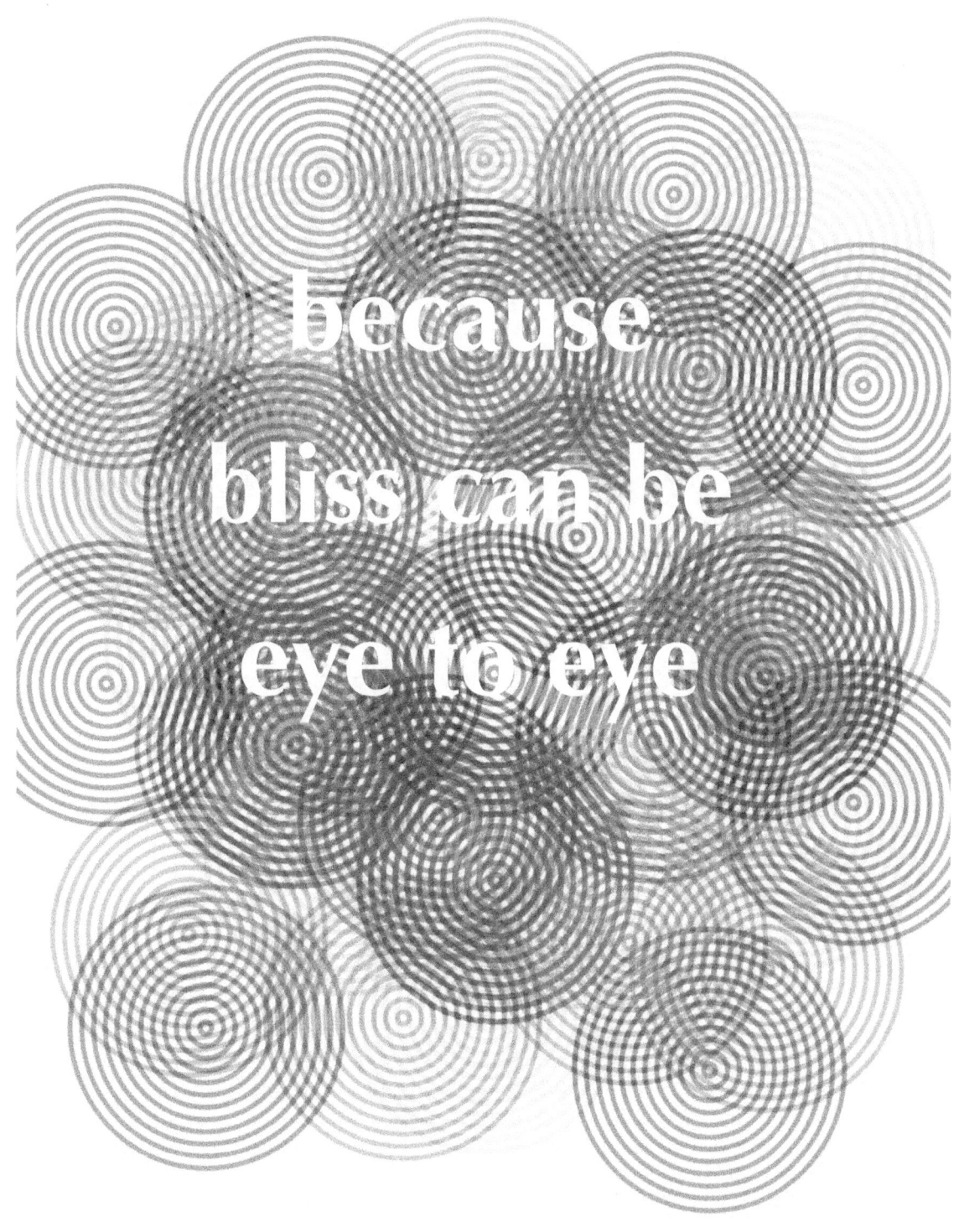

because

bliss can be

eye to eye

before the

Big Bang

there was only a

book of matches

resting on a

lounge chair

in Florida

fostering a
hygienic
relationship
to feeling

between
sleep and waking
there's mostly
not-here,
then again,
the essentially
everywhere

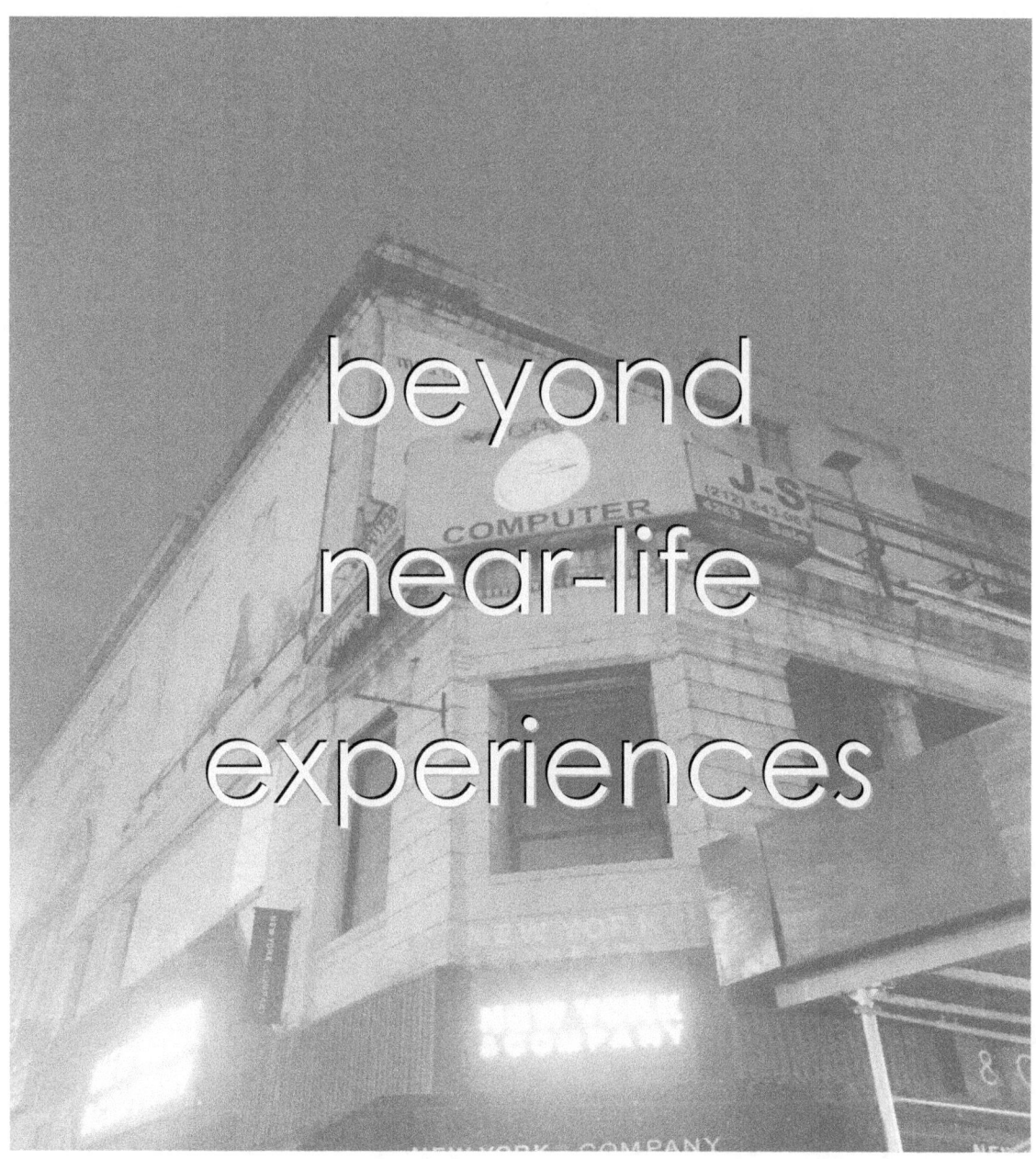

beyond
near-life
experiences

blue

shivers

biting

your own

tail ?

bodily
traces

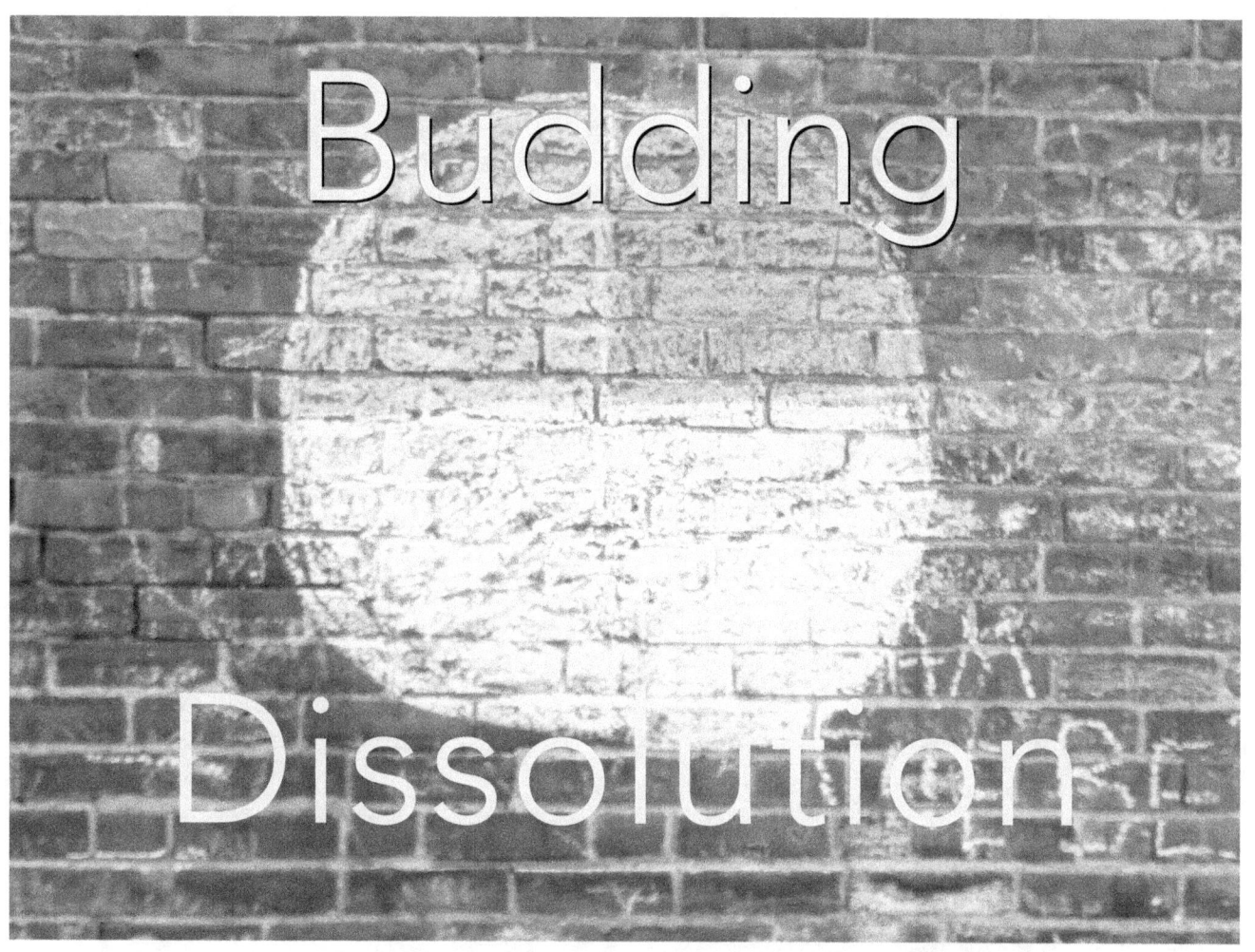

but
the world
has already
ended

c'est la vie with regard to virtual transparency

wading

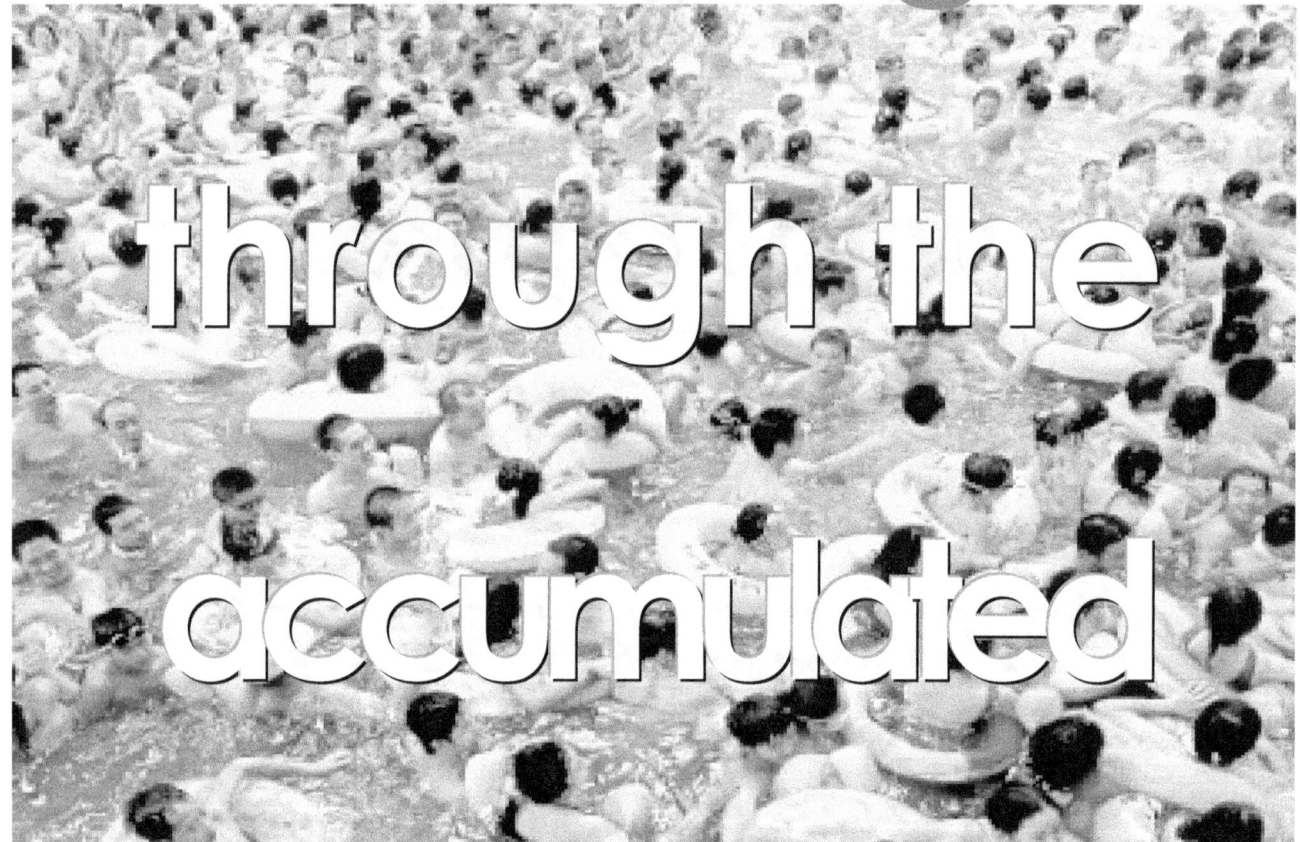

through the

accumulated

superficiality

 character refuses

deceit

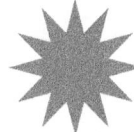

c^{ir}c_ul_ar

in_sp_{ir}ation

claim
listening

no matter what

color

is

as

color

does

in the spirit of trusteeship
instead of the current
political deal let's have
everyone in Congress
handcuffed together
all day, everyday

consciousness

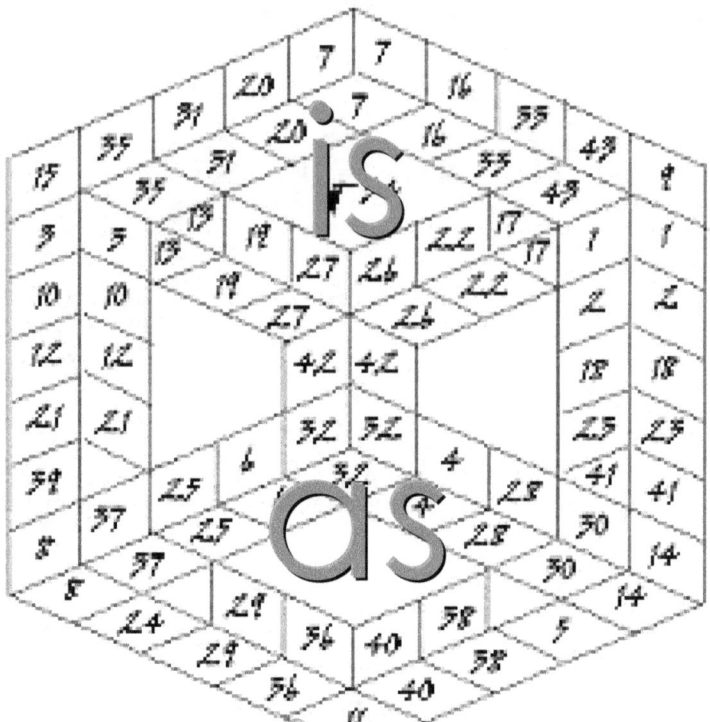

is

as

consciousness

does

consider
destiny
beginning
in your
fingertips

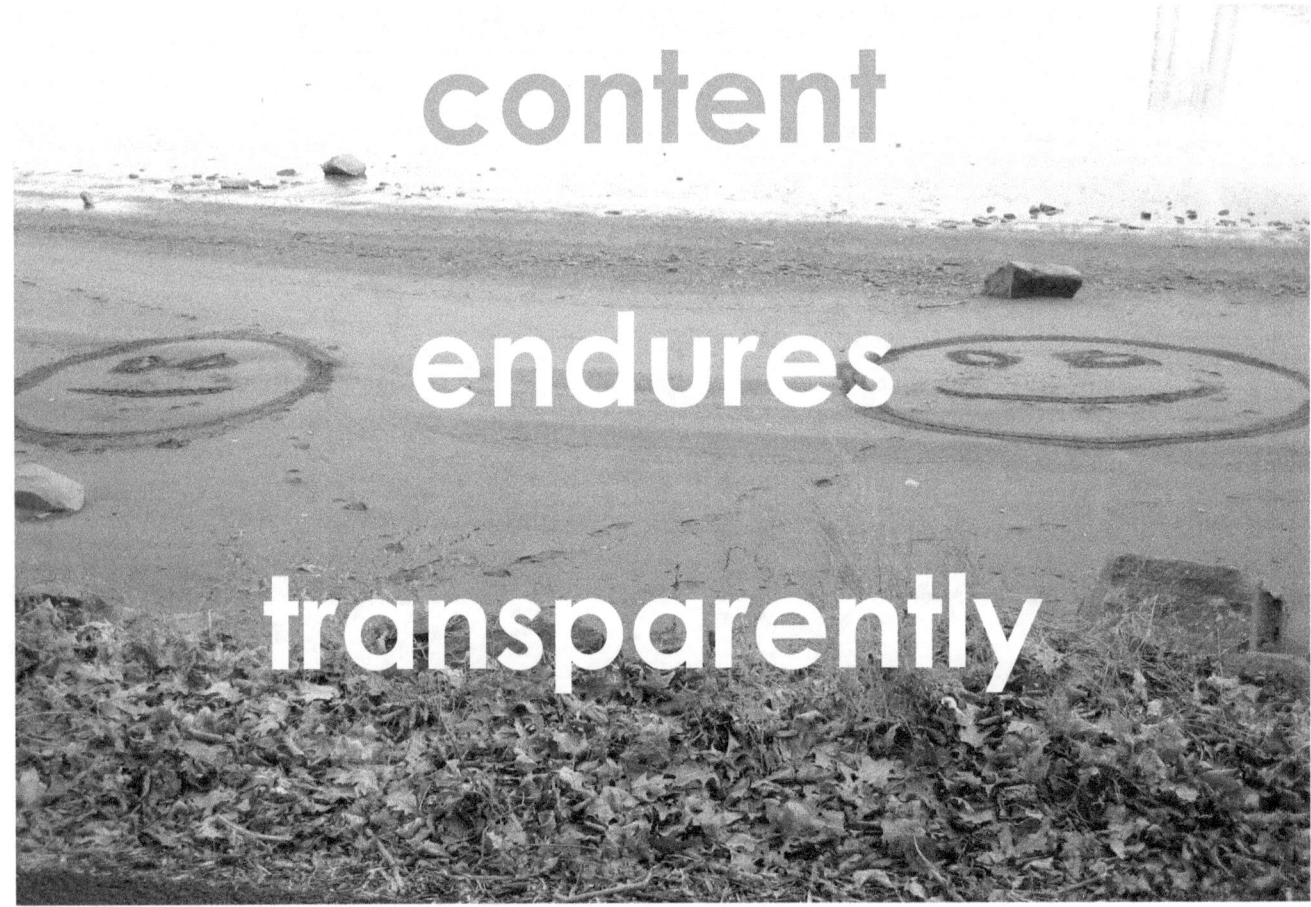

content

endures

transparently

created to

fulfill the dream

of

free

consent

culture

ended

with our

consent

Culture is a display of
ideation
soaked in a crystal coffin,
appreciated and fondled
through recombinant forces
of egotism,
then sold for
$ $ $ $

dancing through unseen influences

DANGER: Things Evolve

You've Arrived!

With Appropriate Attitude
& Lofty Aspirations

Without a Hint of Regret or
Disappointment

You've Arrived!

destiny
takes
account of
there
being no
addendum
to eternity

dissonance
is the new
harmony

if gravity is

acceleration

levity

is surrender

don't you

wanna

die

healthy?

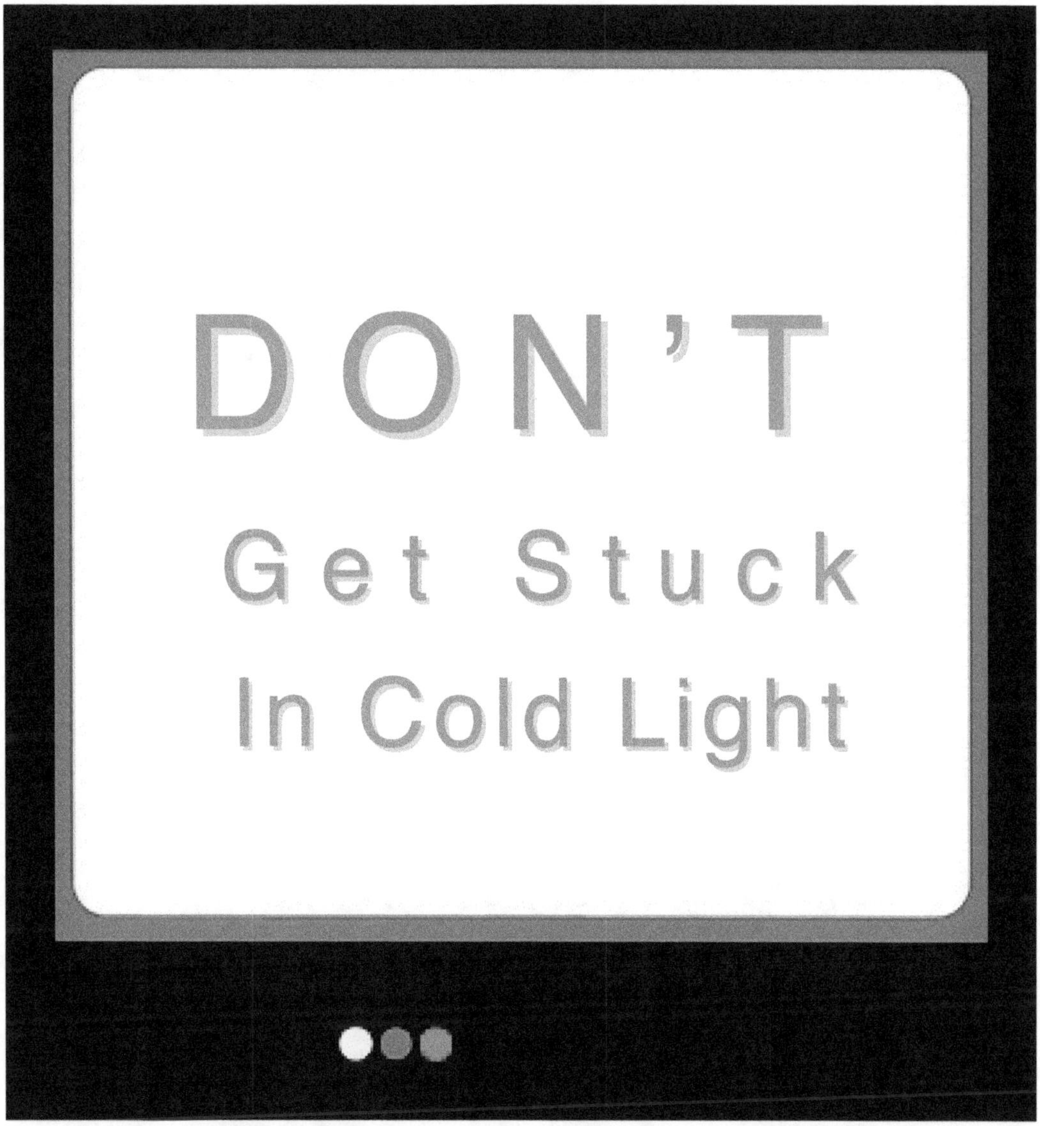
DON'T
Get Stuck
In Cold Light

don't put off
till your next
incarnation
what you can
accomplish
IN THIS ONE

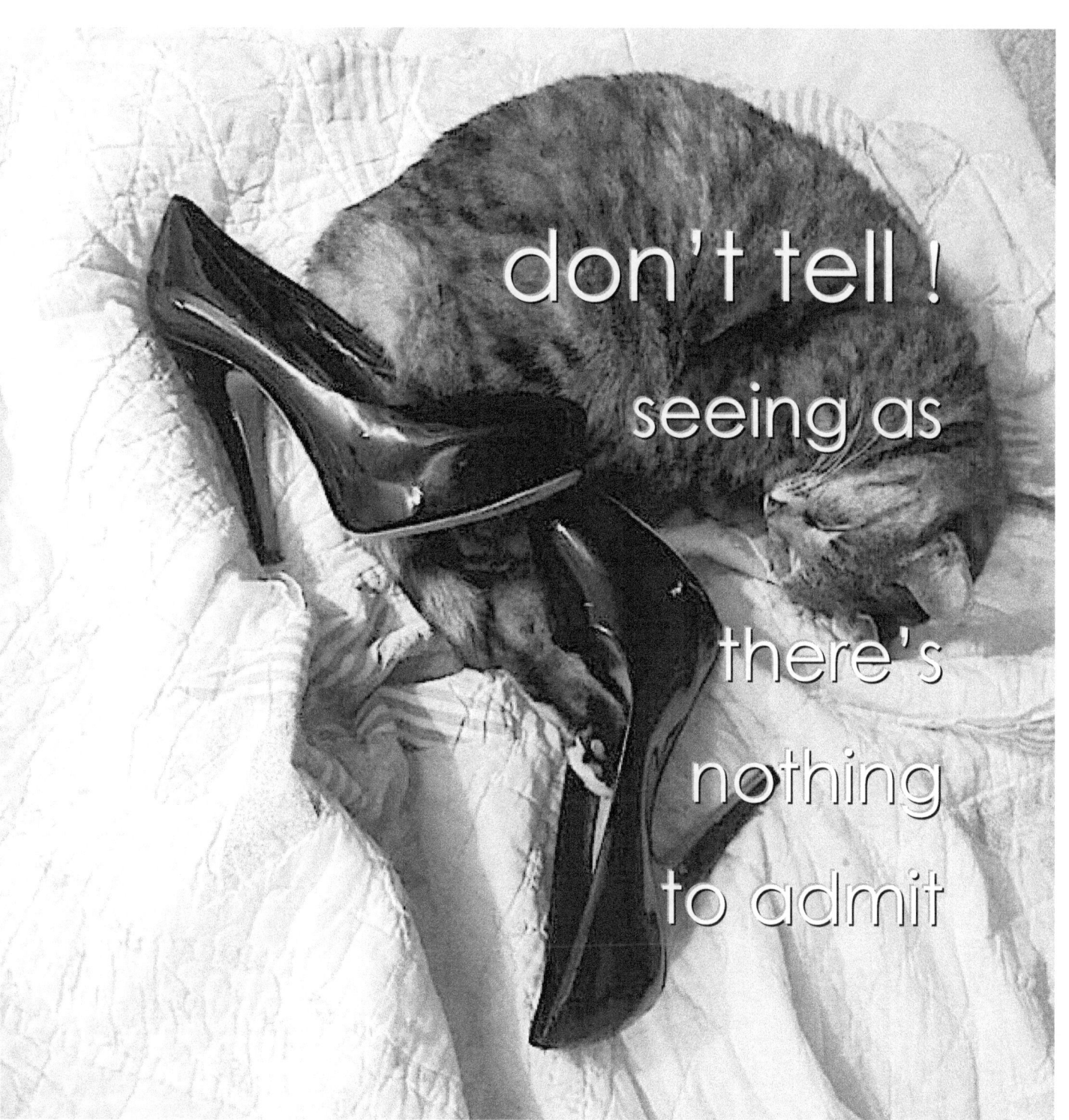

don't tell !

seeing as

there's

nothing

to admit

69

doppelgänger

doppelgänger

FREEING

OBJECTS

FROM YOUR

RESENTMENT
S

friends
are
poisoned
by similar
forces

from
one lifetime
to the
next

:-)

function is
essentially
dependent upon
extinguishing or
stoking a flame

giving a
go at
civilization
are we?

global

magic

intrigue

gosh,
that's a
joyful
tongue!

habits
display
truisms...
but about
what?

Facial

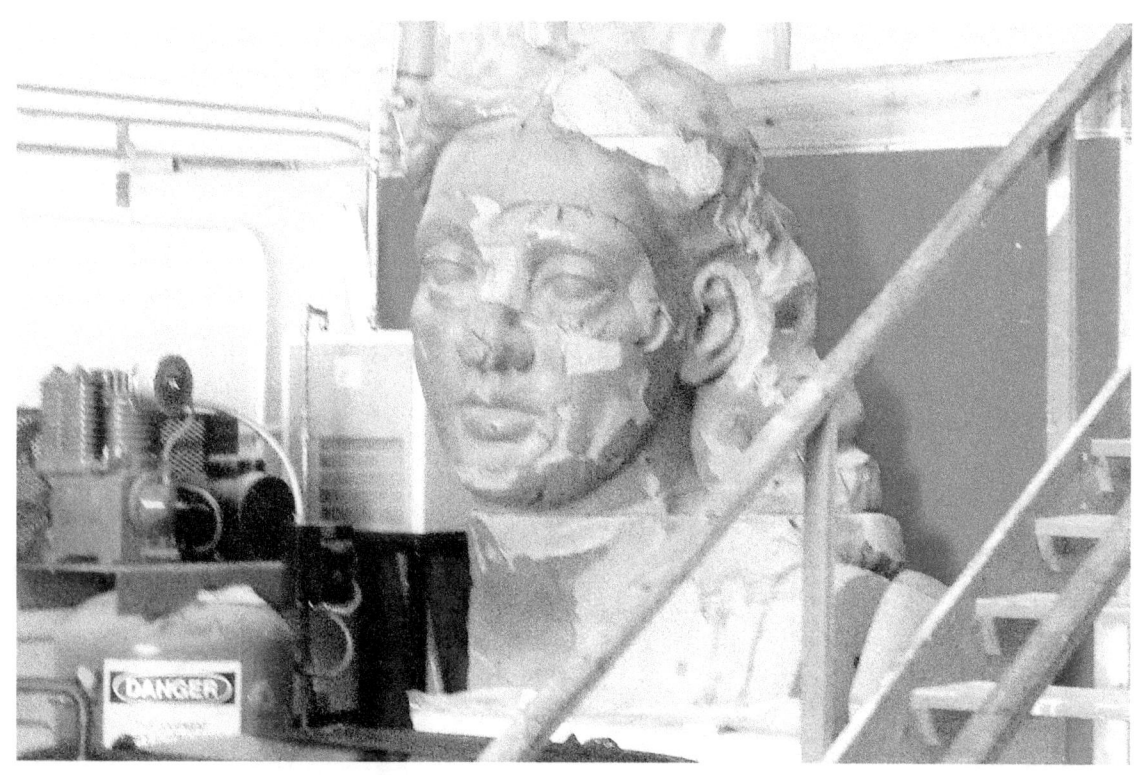

Vibe

happiness
is a
liquid...
love is
a gas

hard as they
come,
heads are never
square

sex became
the psyche's
original spin

have no
opinions?

**the inverted image of
the universe**

wants to hear
from you!

headless,

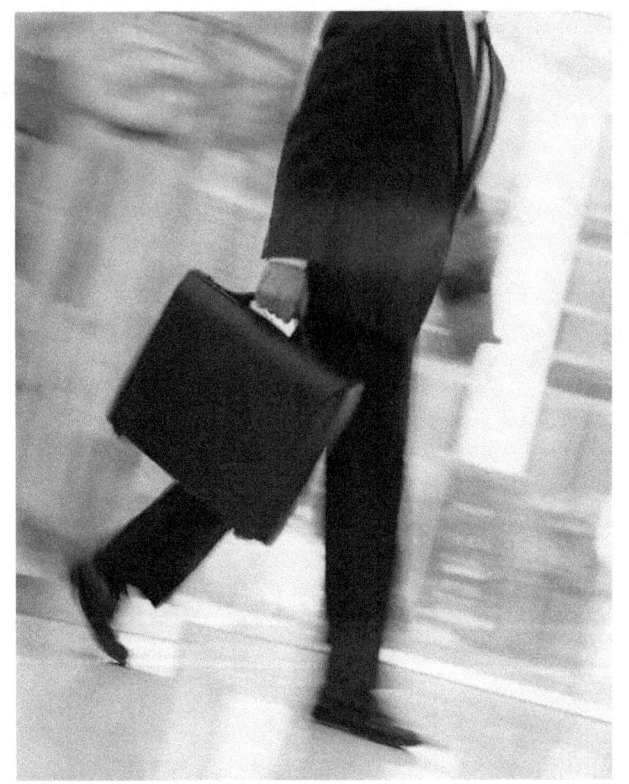

& loving it!

⌒∠⊙≡≈∽∧◎「◇△▽¤

Heavenly Measures

⌒∠⊙◎≈∽∧「◇≡△▽¤

heavenly measures

∠⊙△≡≈∽∧◎⌒「◇▽¤

heavenly pleasures

⌒∠◇「⊙≡¤∽≈∧◎△▽

Heavenly Measures

⌒∠⊙≡≈∽∧◎「◇△▽¤

depth sensitive

in the elastic sense

here beauty

& perception

connect

cosmic fact

history is
divine nature
in the throes of a
psychotic event

Life:

a sphere

swelling opaque,

centripetally

shrinking

hmm, how 'bout working on your personality?

how did the
mentality begin,
the one that generates
treatment solely by

ADDRESSING
SYMPTOMS?

how is **my** **attitude** ruining my **worth?**

humor
trumps
the lot

you may not
know anything
about your
death...

but you're not
separate from
your death

if beauty can be
on the *inside*,
what enables it to
be on the *outside*?

if
we agree
to this reality
we really
ought to have
MORE FUN

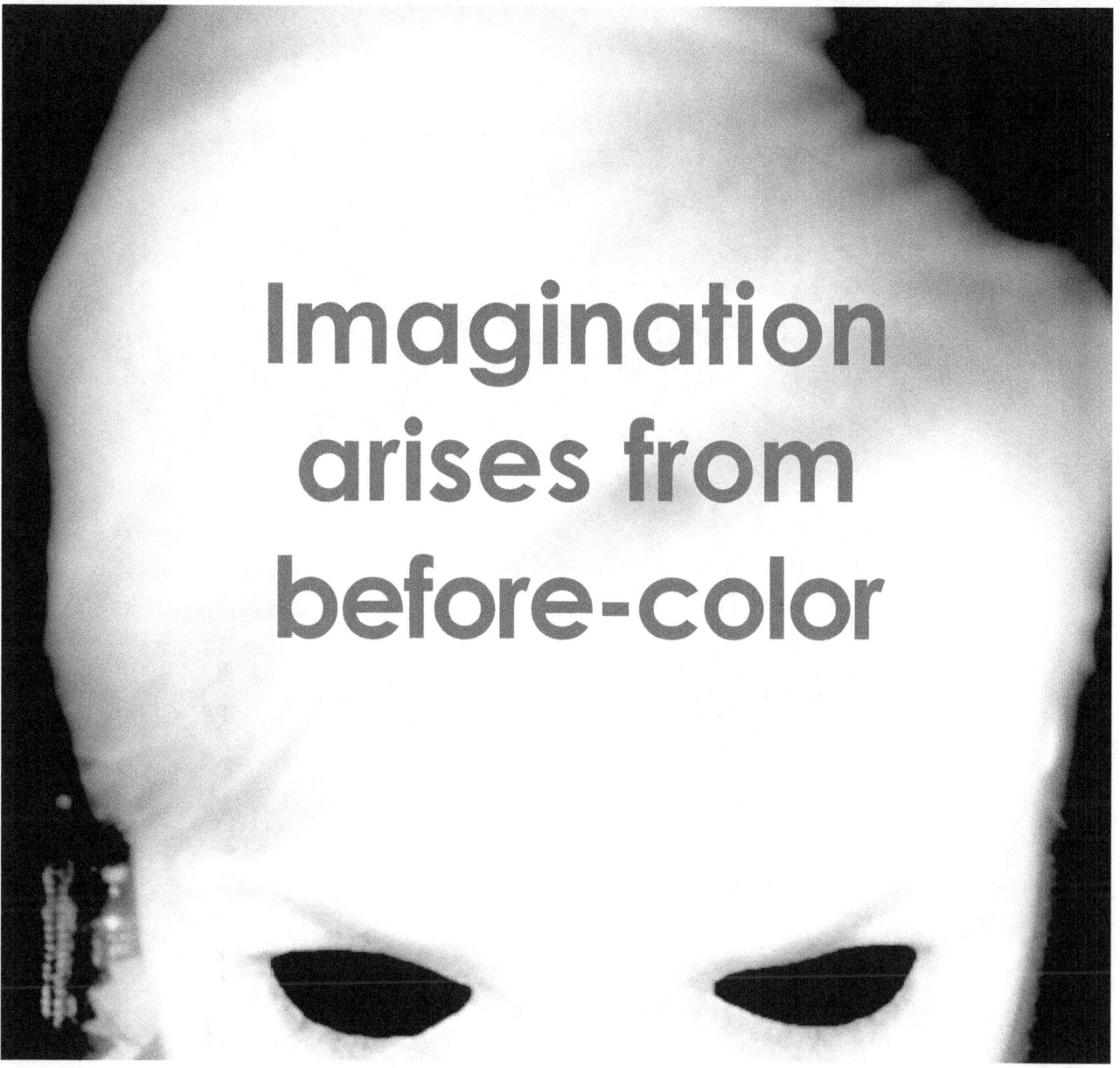

Imagination arises from before-color

imbued with filthy

distractions

to embody an

immaculate concentrate

in the
beginning
there was
attitude

in the
discord
of
spiritland

Ocular Communion:

the everyday monstrance of found objects

In the Role of Companionship

Pets Are Commonly Enrolled To Avoid Encountering Ourselves

In This Air
a Body Does
Not Fall

individually gathered

identity difference

Infinity warrants the clarifying of YOU

initialized by
the senses,
two parts
are born

Inside you is a thought you cannot think.

You cannot think of it,

and it forgives you infinitely.

inspired knottiness
brings out the very
best hypotheses

an afflatus is a rush of unexpected breath,

a powerful force or a blow

rendering the recipient

helpless

Inwardly,
think
outside
the body

it's been a
luminous
day's
night

it's never too early
to plan an
after-death learning
program

it's **not** what you think, it's what you *don't* think

listen to …

Taste

:

liberation through invisible art

light is sexy;
glowing in
the dark is
s e x i e r

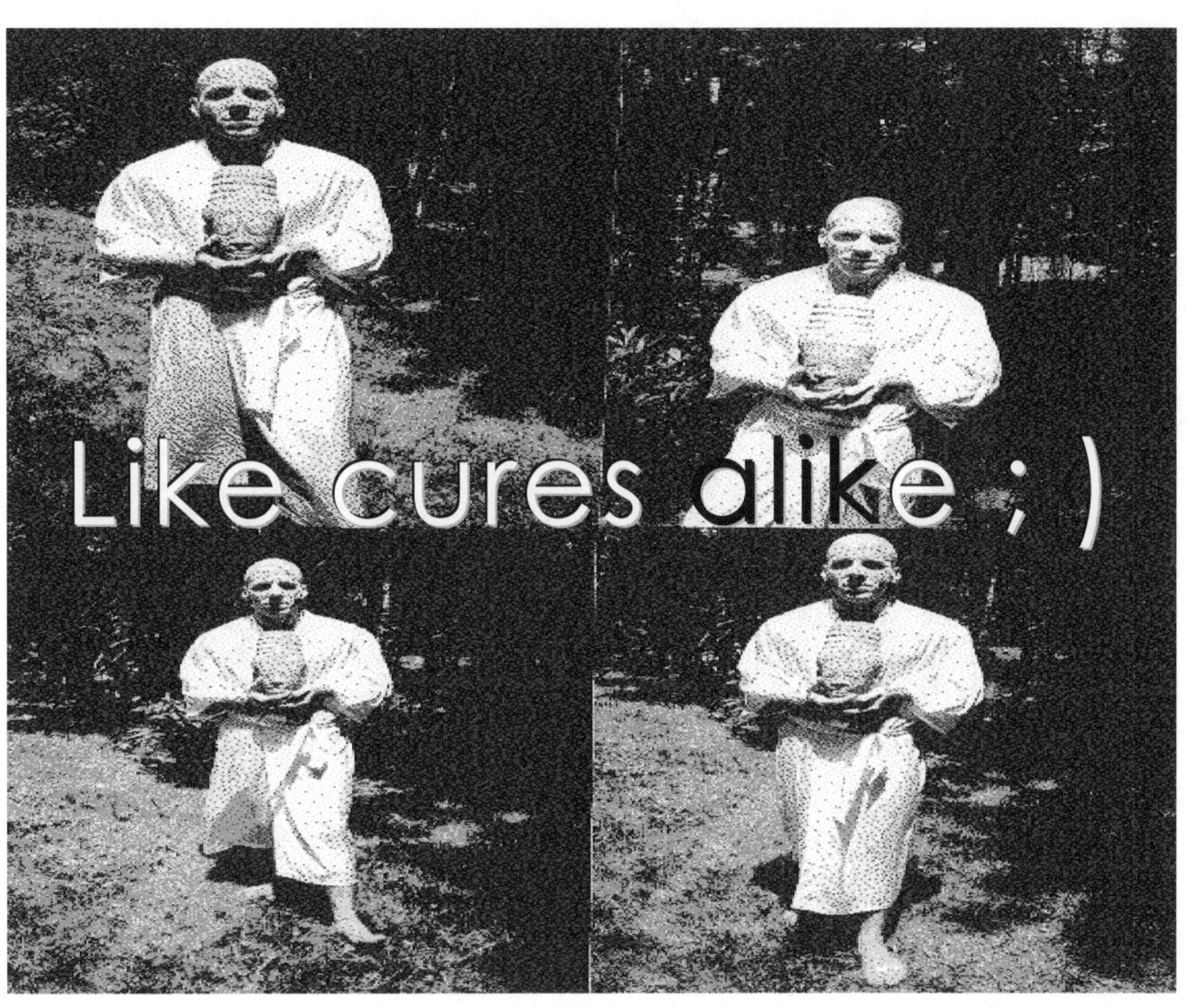

Like cures alike ;)

like music

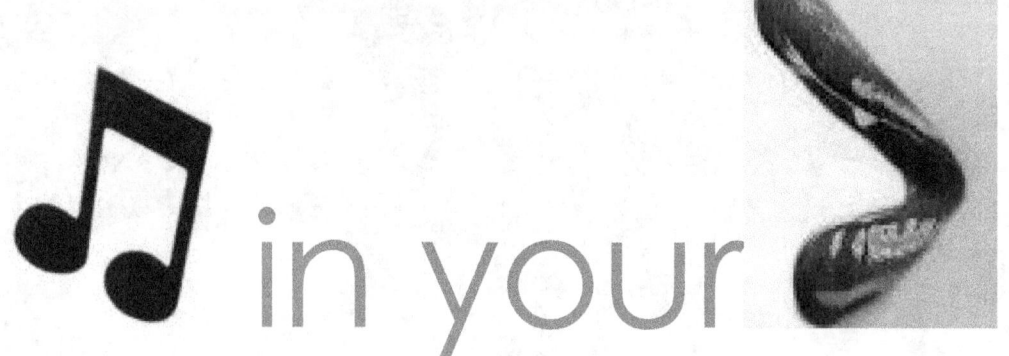

in your

mouth

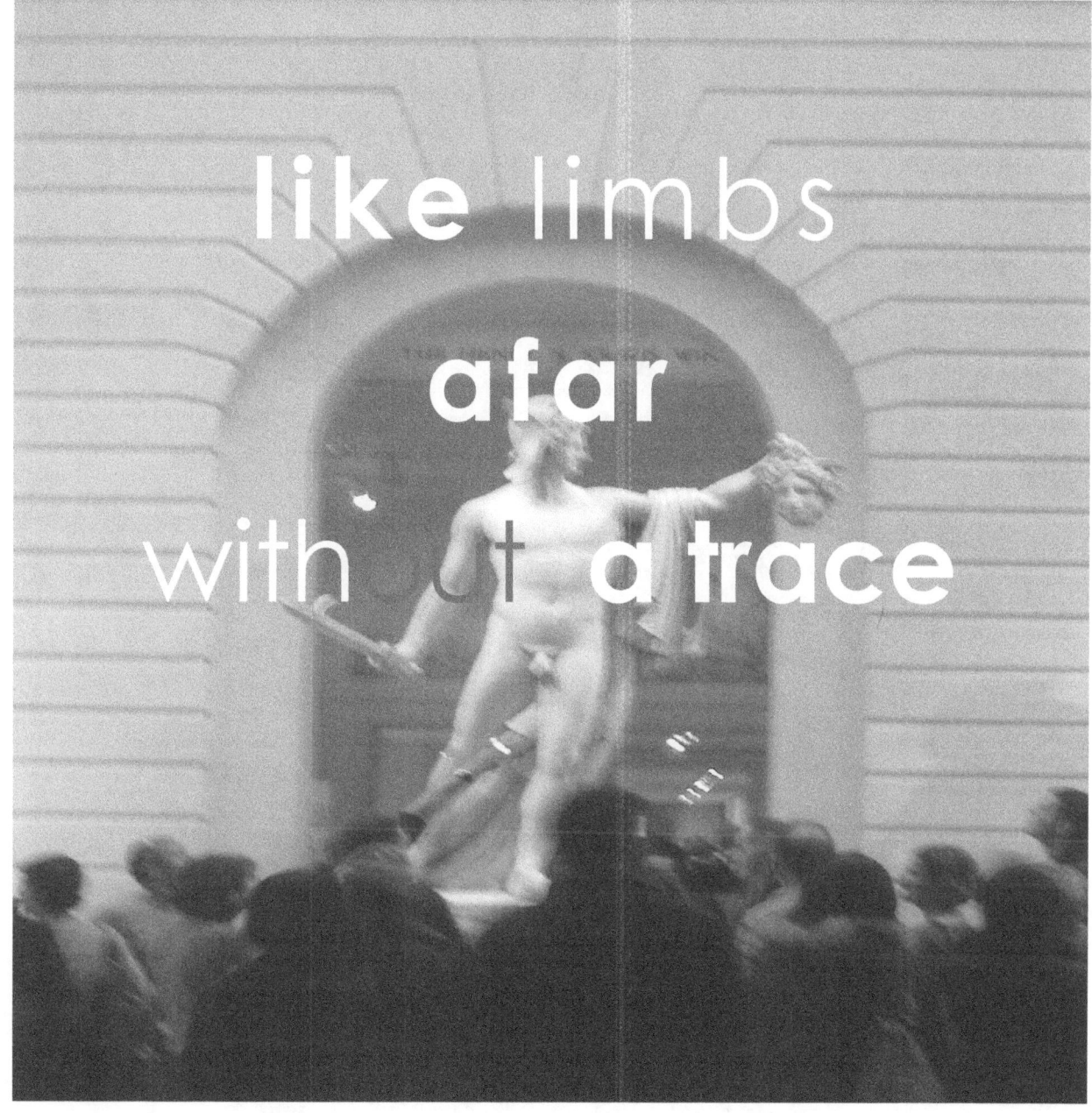

like limbs afar without a trace

living in the
aftermath
in the dream
of spirits

love → assembling pra L aya

love → assembling

→ assembling pra L aya love → assembling

love → assembling pra L aya

love → assembling

assembling pra L aya

Love

Cascade

lush post-
miminalism
& wry fortitude

M – A – N – T – R – **A – R – T** – N – A – M

M – A – N – T – R – A – R – T – N – A – M

M – A – N – T – R – A

A – R – T – N – A – M

M – A – N – **T – R** – A – R – T – N – A – M

M – A – N – T – R – **A – R** – T – N – A – M

metabolism

is of the

future

mis-consciousness

mis-consciousness

mis-consciousness

mis-consciousness

mis-consciousness

mis-consciousness

mis-consciousness

mis-consciousness

a replica

Moment

make a

M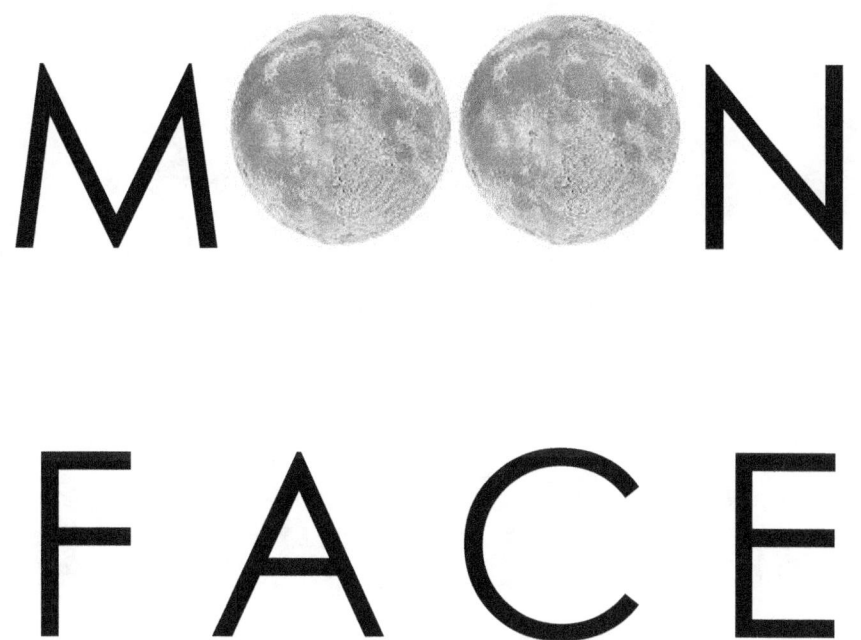N

FACE

movement

lies ahead

of the

physical body

in the moment

feeling pursuing

by the sonic contours of the will

& the other way around

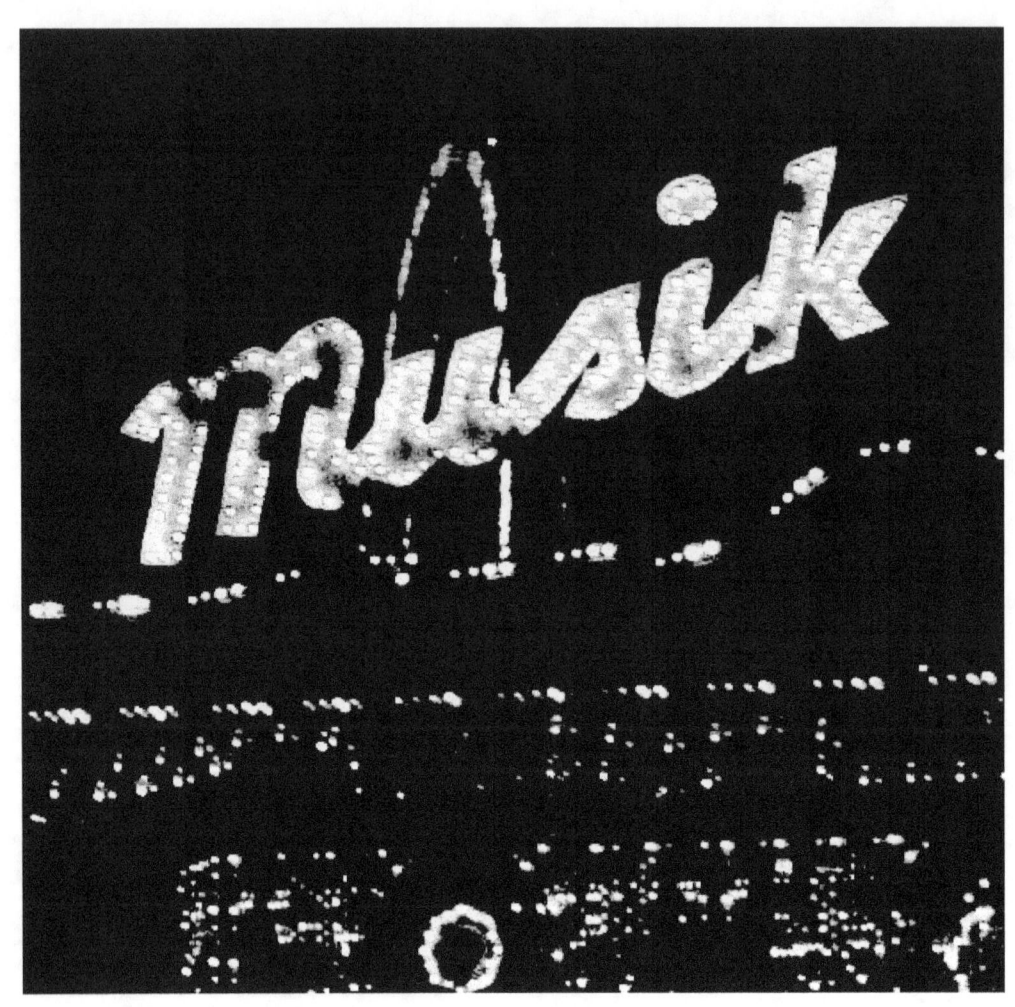

refuses to lie

need silence?

_____?

new ways
to disarm
the small-
hearted

no matter what,

insist on...

nobody's
a prophet in their
homeland,
but everyone's
a mystic
on the crapper

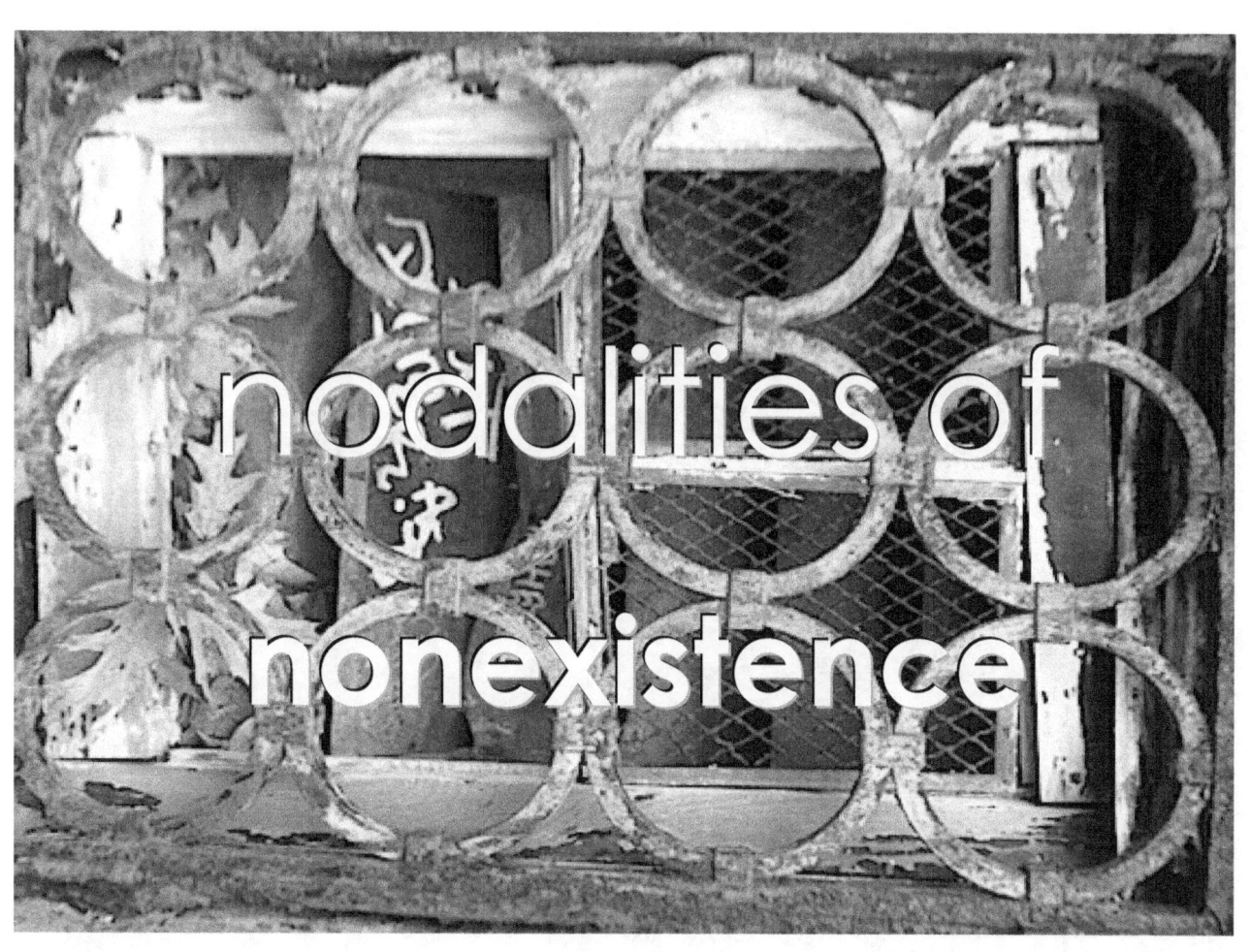

nodalities of
nonexistence

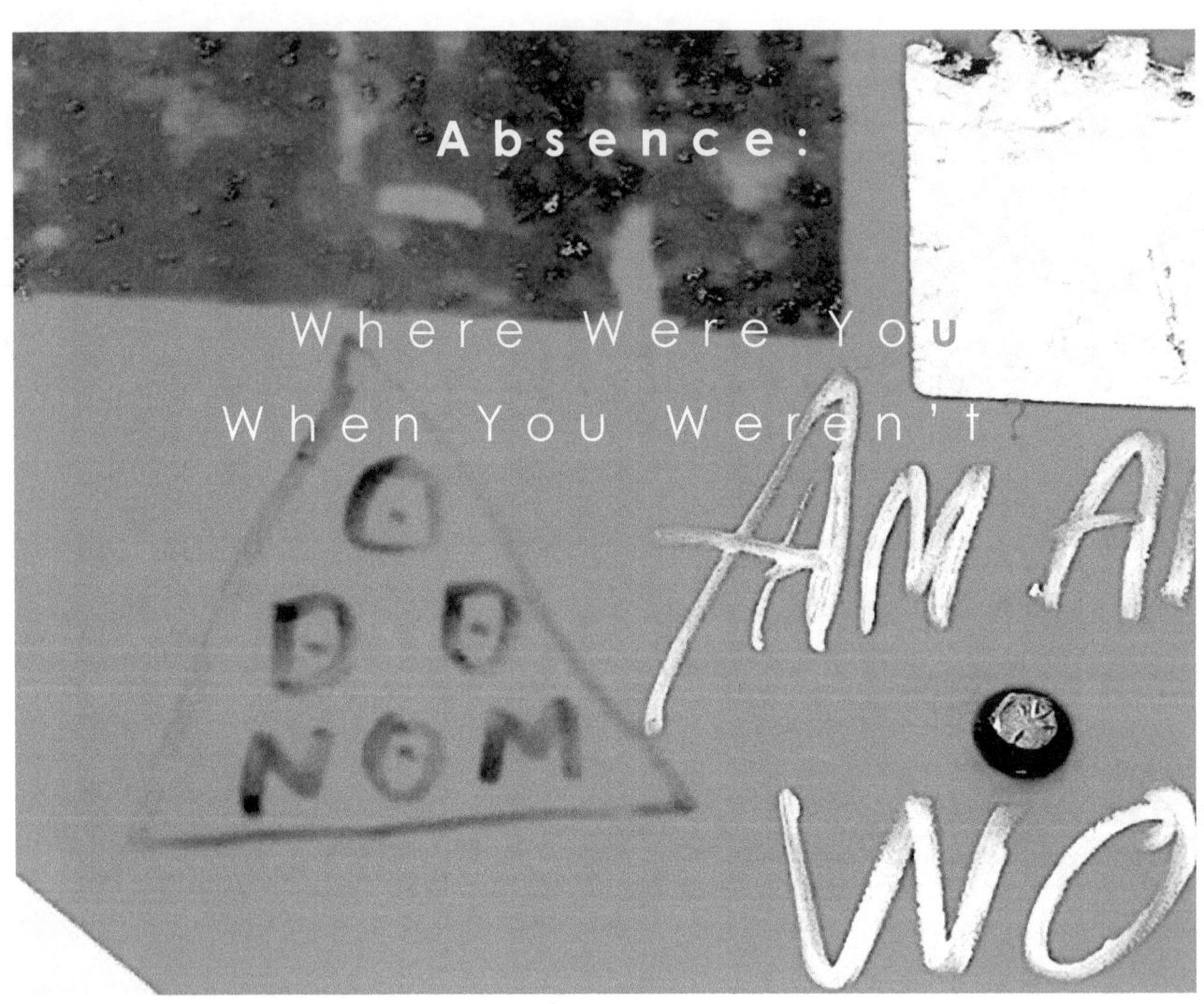

Absence:

Where Were You

When You Weren't

nothing is seen

observe the lack
of character in
monsters
and excuses

Occupy
Yourself
and the totality of
Your Omissions

occupy yourself & the totality of your conditions

occupy yourself & the totality of your decisions

politics &
big
pharma:
one hand
dirtying the
other

ontology in your face

our ancestors
follow us
wherever we
go...
hoping we'll
surprise them

PARADISE
ALL OVER

perception fastens the world centrifugally

sensation envelops the world centripetally

PHENOMENA THEMSELVES ARE THEORY-LADEN

physical nature, ethereal nature, the subtleties of movement & nuances of change, celestial resistance, cosmological conundrums

physiognomy
is sure to one
day reveal
culpability

poetry is the divine

searching about

in your throat

music longs to
reveal what cannot
be heard

poetry yearns to
utter what cannot
be said

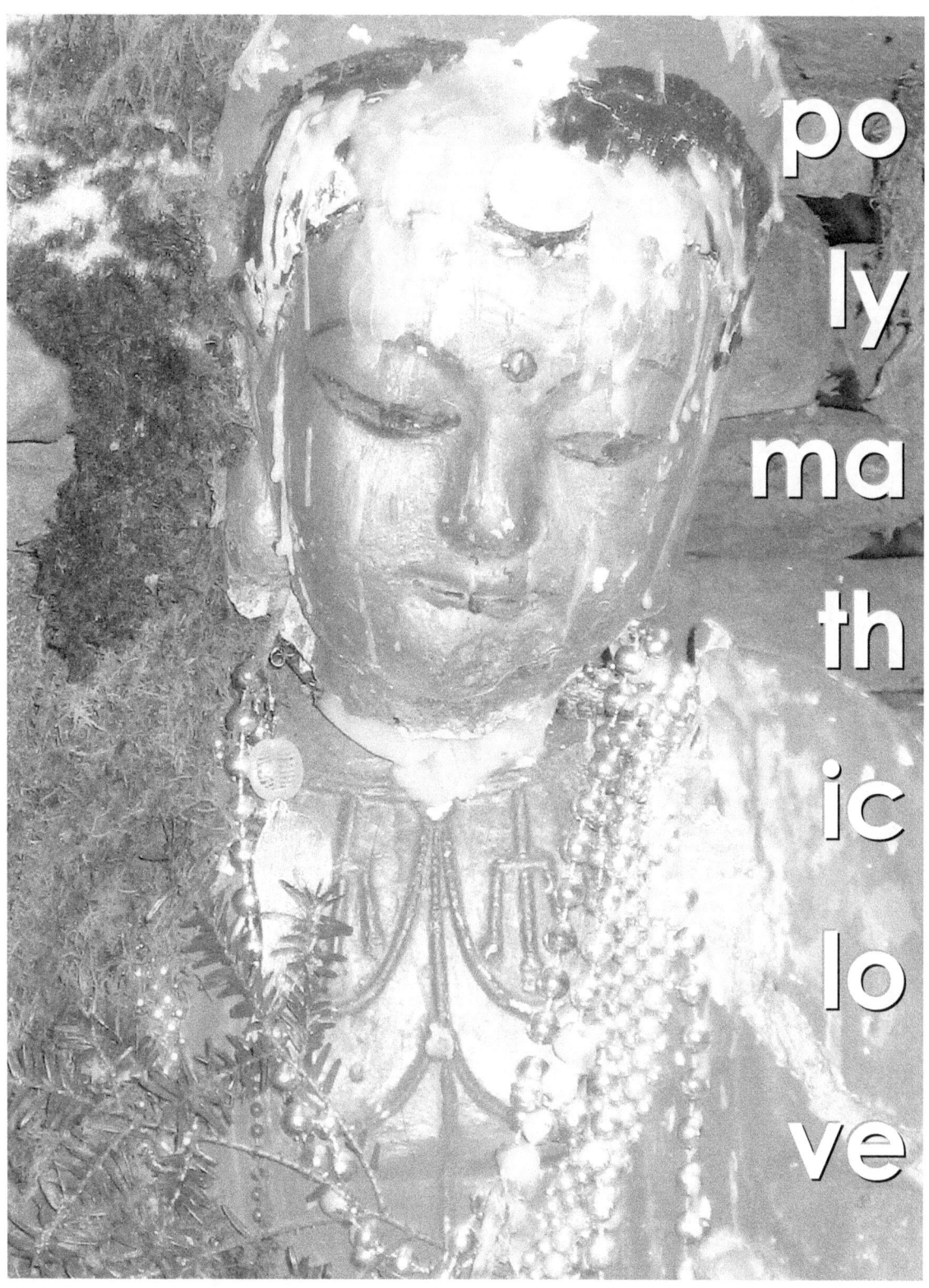

po
ly
ma
th
ic
lo
ve

153

luminosity = successful enthusiasm

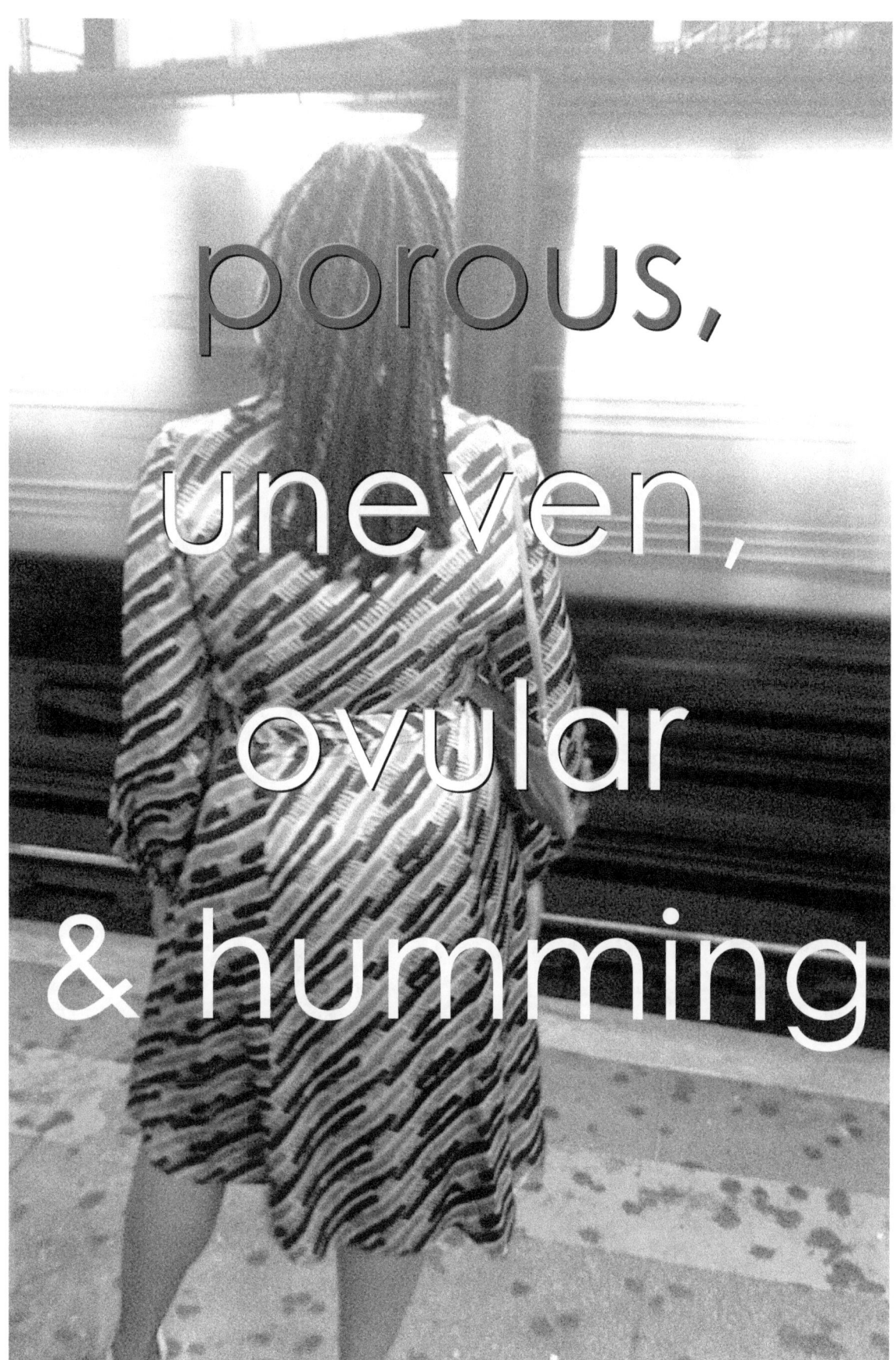

porous,
uneven,
ovular
& humming

a precondition for immortality?

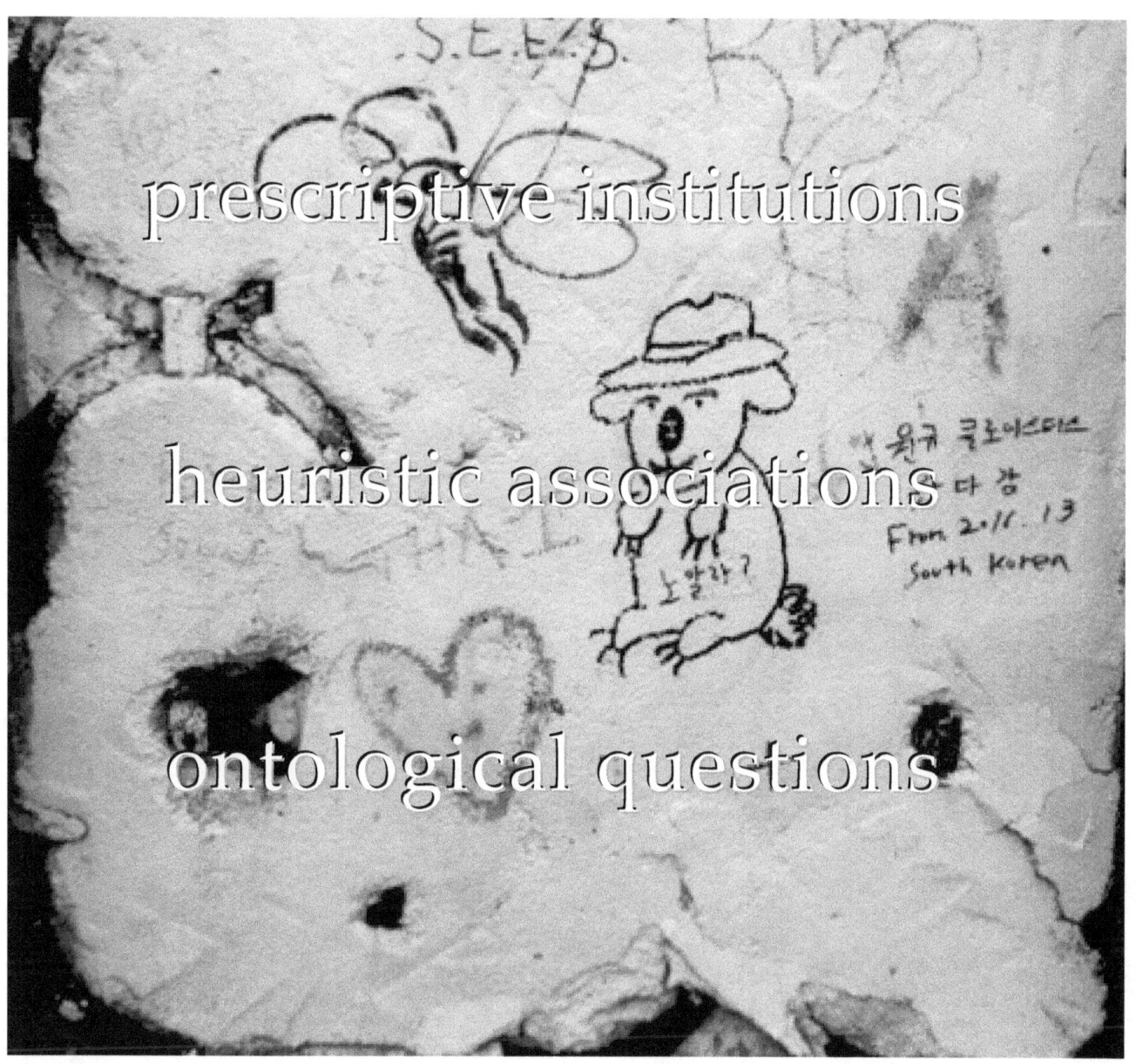

prescriptive institutions

heuristic associations

ontological questions

primal
warmth sets up
the archetypal
beginning —
the condition for
YOU & ANOTHER

PROBLEMS ARE NOT THE PROBLEM

PROBLEMS ARE NOT THE PROBLEM

PROBLEMS ARE NOT THE PROBLEM

PROBLEMS ARE NOT THE PROBLEM

PROBLEMS ARE NOT THE PROBLEM

PROBLEMS ARE NOT THE PROBLEM

PROBLEMS ARE NOT THE PROBLEM

PROBLEMS ARE NOT THE PROBLEM

projections
are not always
projections

Projective Mythology and Tactile Imagination

projective mythology & tactile imagination

projective mythology & tactile imagination

Projective Mythology and Tactile Imagination

rescuing the digital world

IS part of

evolution

reverence

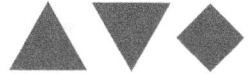

gratitude

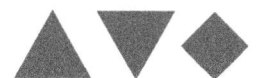

devotion

risk & play

effort & fortuity

ritualizing philosophy?

mythologizing error

SATURN

SUCCUSSION

SATURN

DESCENT

YOU REALLY CAN'T BE "LOST" IN SPACE

seeing through the reservoir of appearances

SenSe

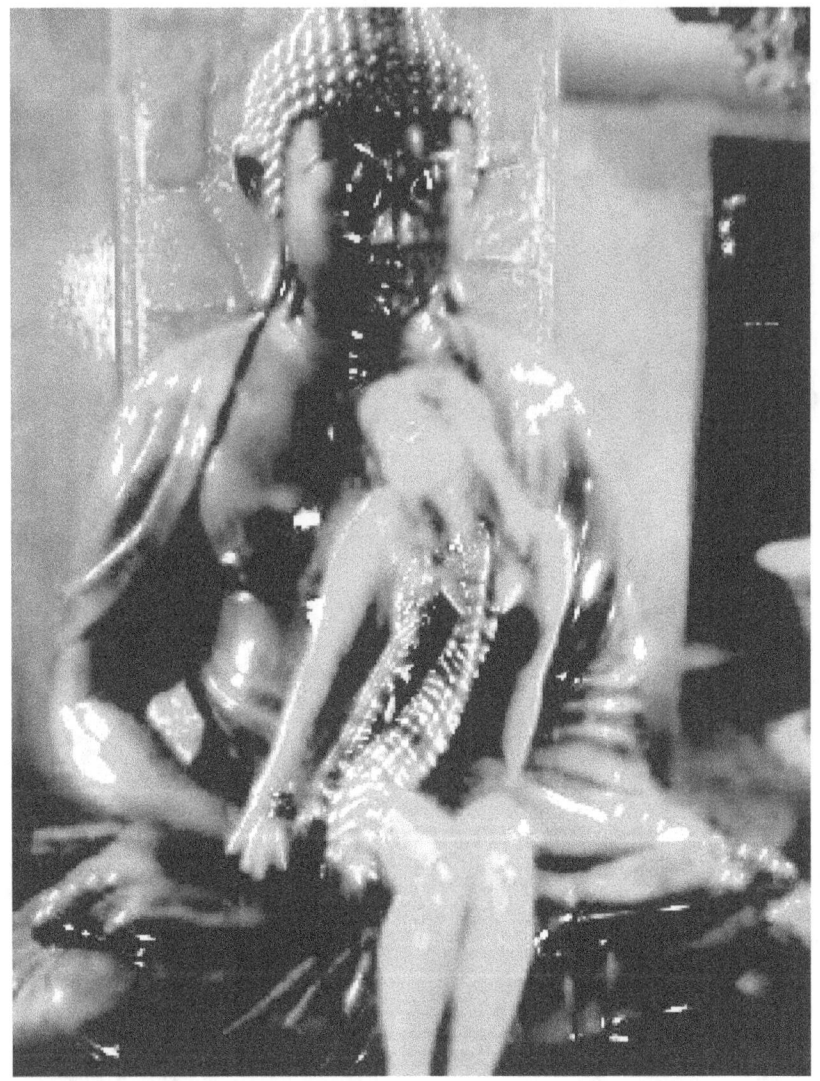

& Surface

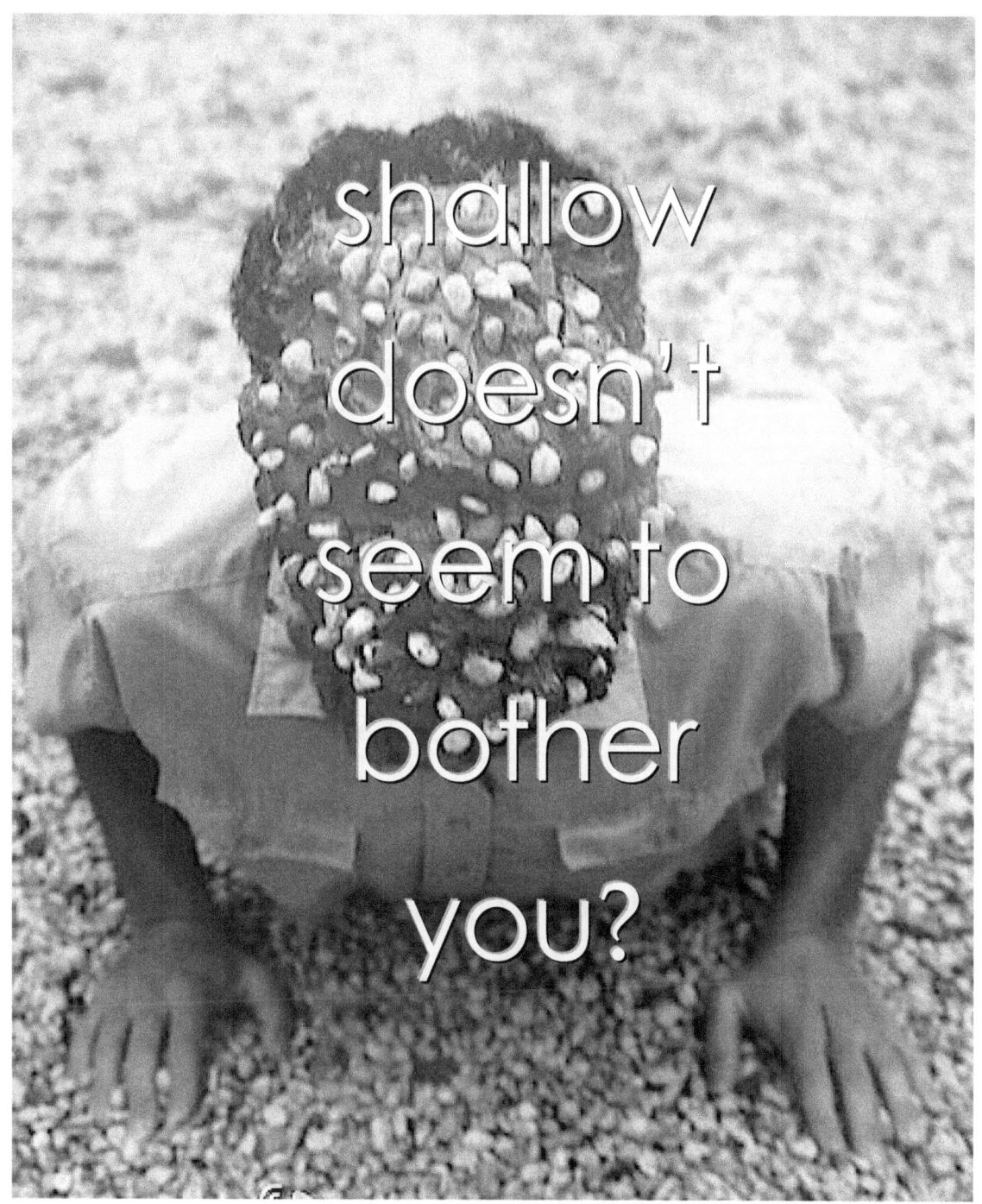

shallow
doesn't
seem to
bother
you?

· · · ·

Share some of your
secrets? Correspond
about invisible art?

Get in touch by

imagining

our breaths

mingling

· · · ·

sharpen it with Buddha

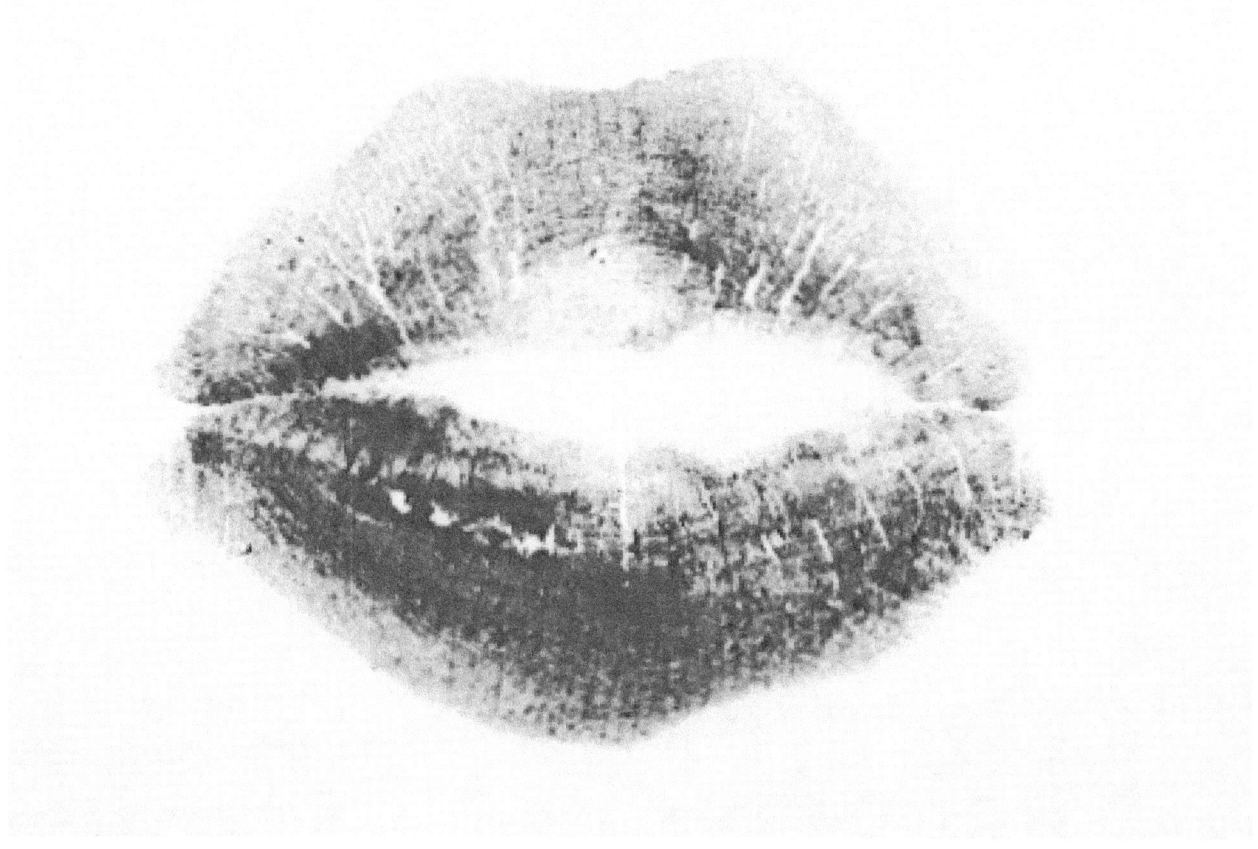

burnish it with Christ

shimmer

Sleep Sleep Sleep

Sleep Sleep Sleep

Sleep Sleep Sleep

9 degrees for exploring out-of-body

Smells

Like

Spirit

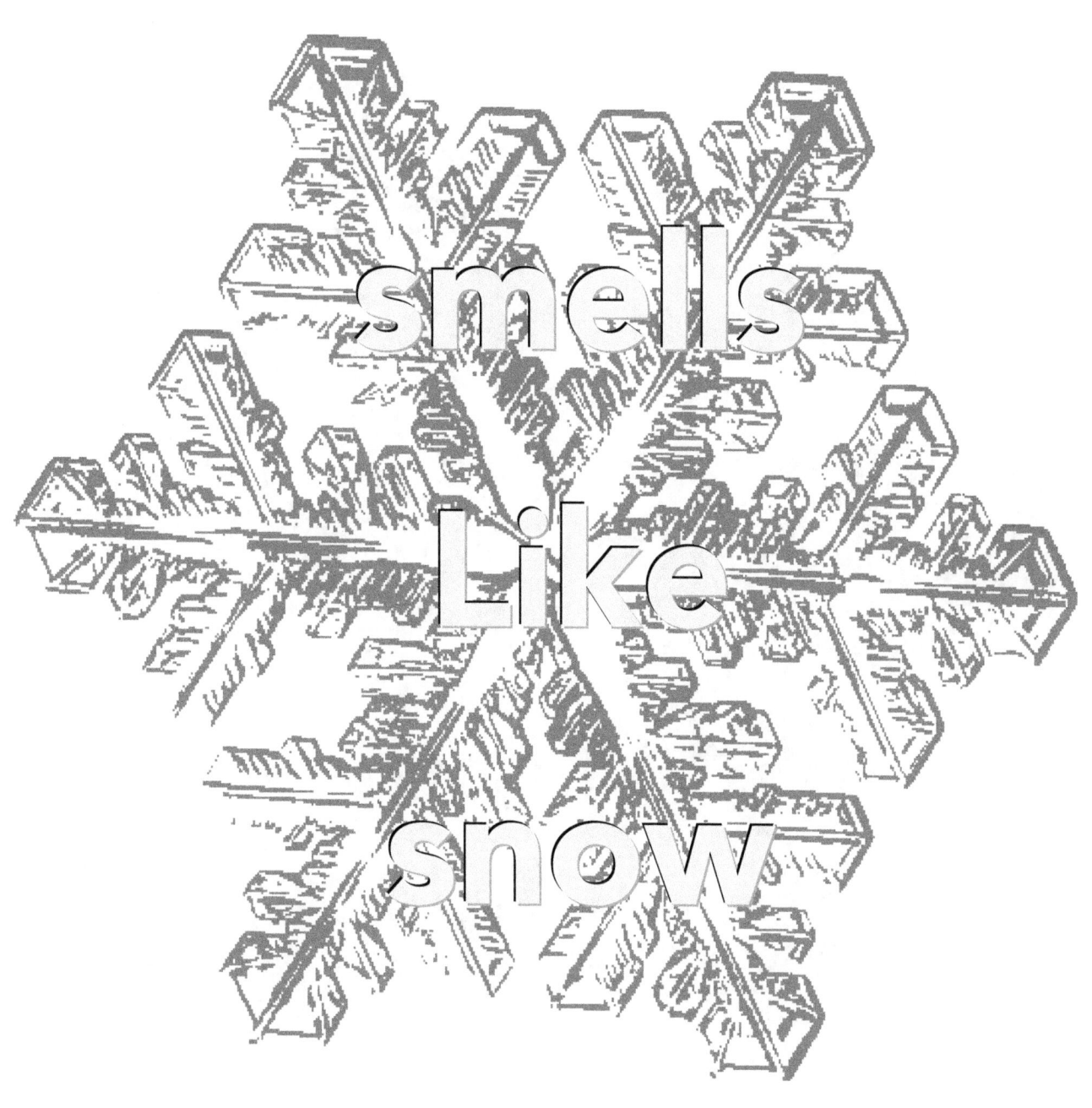

smells
Like
snow

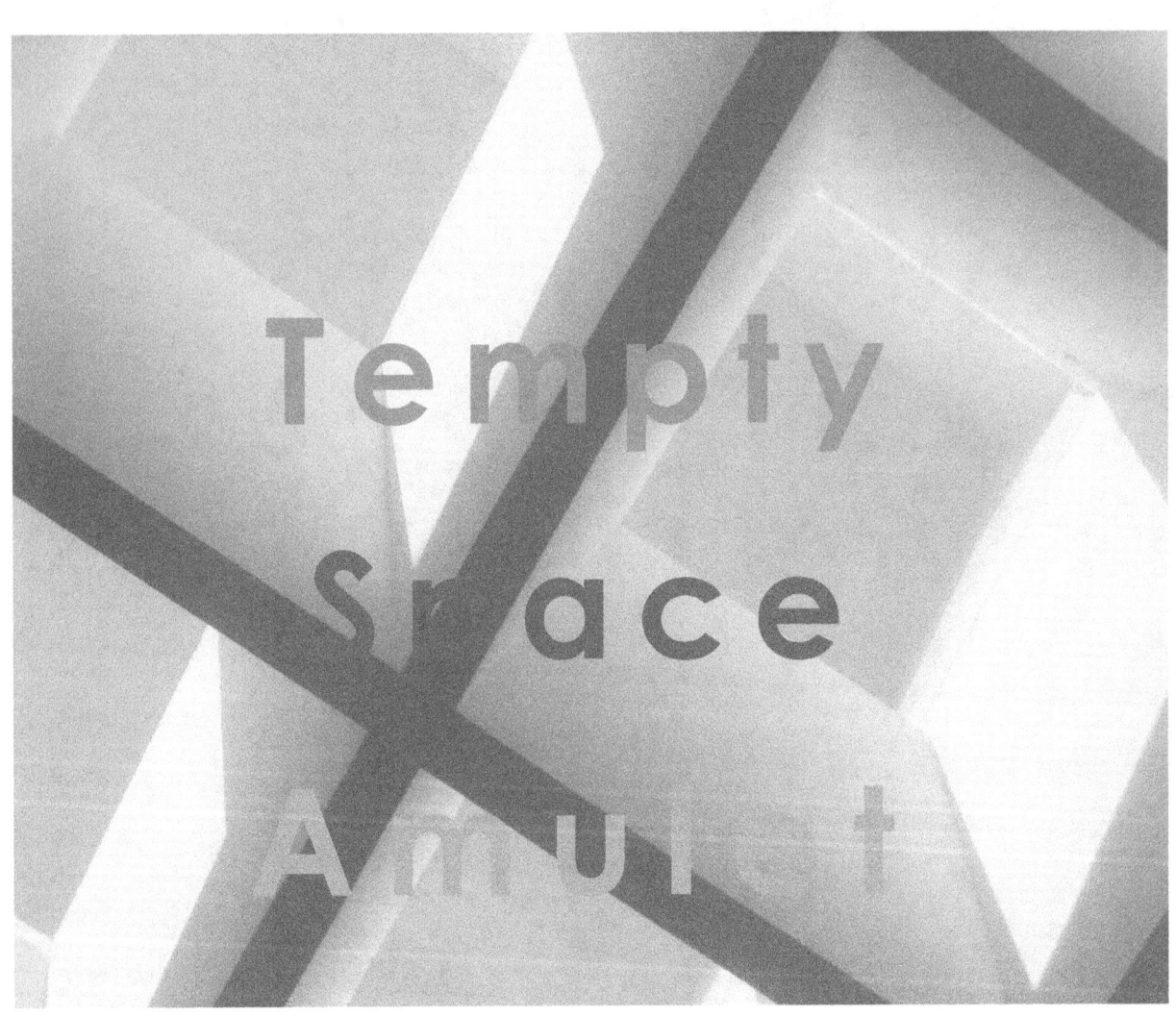

Spiritualizing

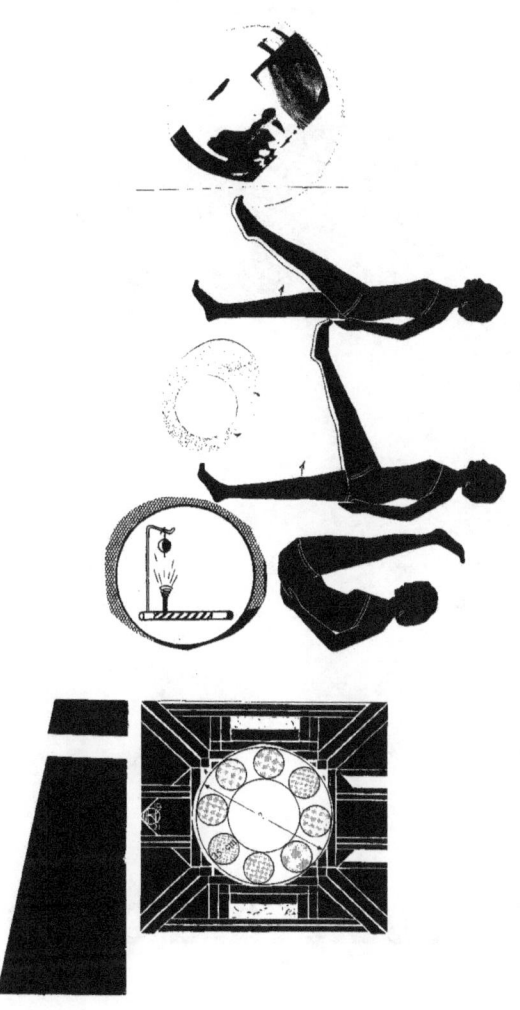

Space

eyelash

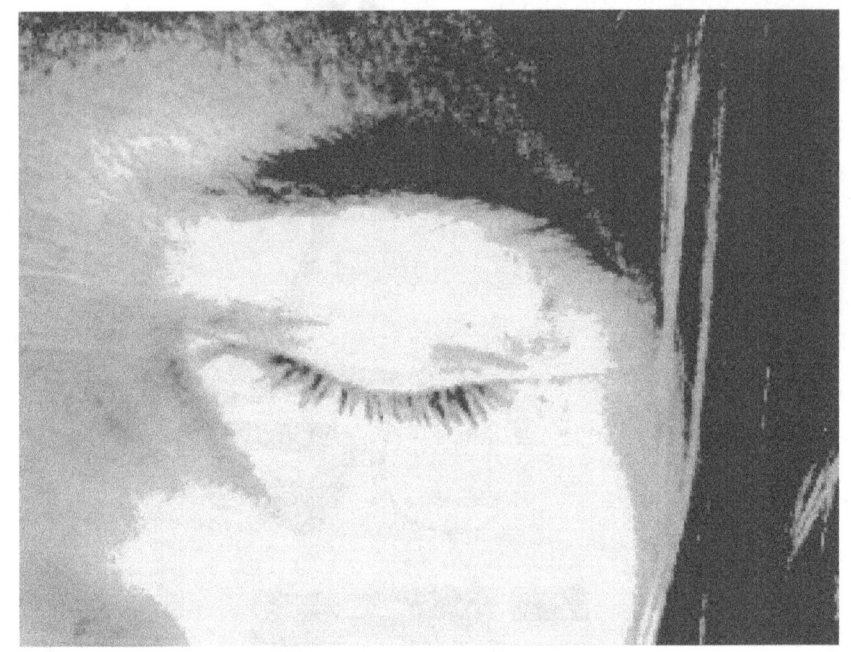

the boulevard of nirvana

sunshine is
destiny,
glare, an
instruction

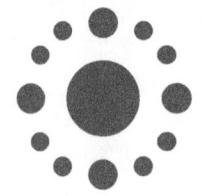

supersensible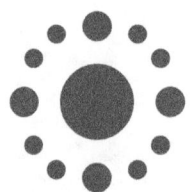

forces

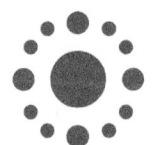

SUSPENSION

taking a
closer look
at less

182

going
deeper,
lightly

take me
into your
cheerfulness

take me,
take me

thinking that
the brain
thinks
is a cliché

The Artist Is No Longer Present:

Aesthetic Sufficiency Through Creative Absence

the
mind is a
dog
smelling its
own butt

The Cesspool Wrought by Religion

the ebullient

gushing forth of

"this is me"

the essence

of smell

unravels

through the

quest

of a lurking

animal

the future

accompanies us

wherever we go

presenting the

dubious promise

that we'll be

caught aware

Imminent is this **messenger** **inhaling** the **not-yet**

the gods are waiting...

to be inspired,

to be reborn

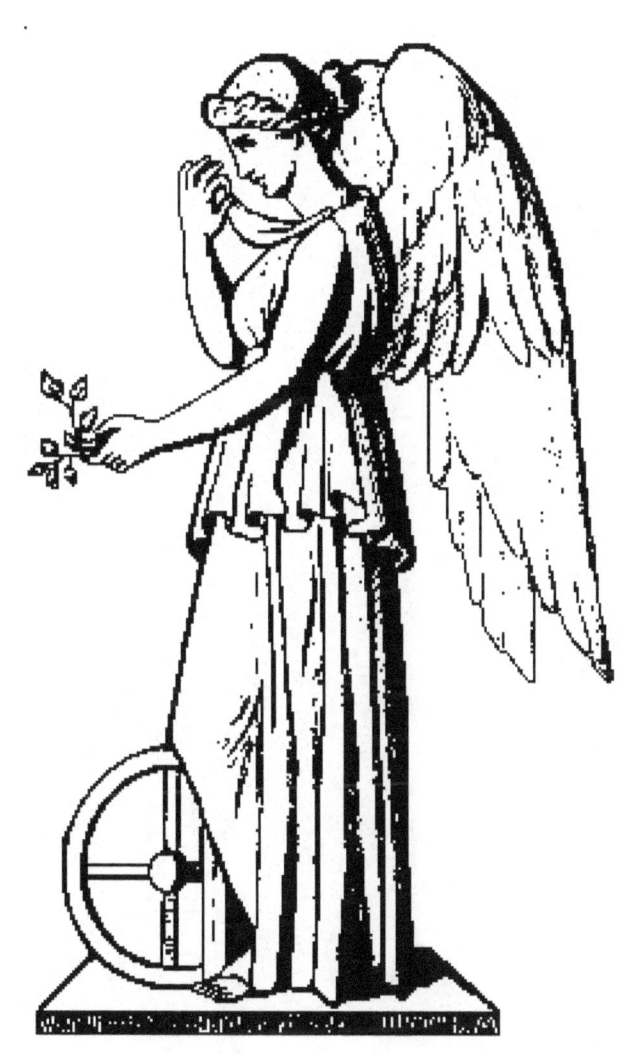

the gods
eat you
if you're
insufferable

the gods

feel our

reflected

mortality

The Great Performance: charming our covenant with time

the greater the need
to vindicate shallowness
of experience, the more
culture is taken with
"creative process"

the **human** stage
goes **through fire**
warmth **and** air,
though fluid ethers
and **mineral**

the issue is not
whether freedom
exists, but that we
can choose
disinterest

"the wonder is not spoiled...
the magic
is not brushed
from the dust
on a butterfly's
wings"

the **magic** of
being physical

all the
misdirected
images

GLOBAL PERFORMANCE OF WORLD-WISDOM VISUALIZED THROUGH YONI MUDRA

Whole Earth Upload honoring Sophia: goddess of wisdom,

World-lover, Dancer and Mother of God

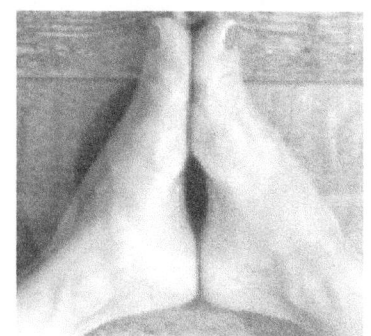 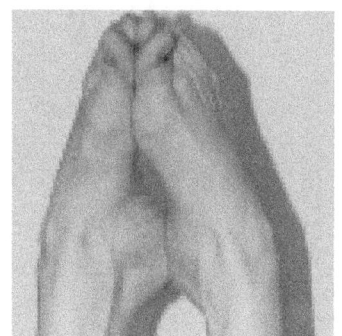

Arches of the feet replicating the World-vagina (inner views)

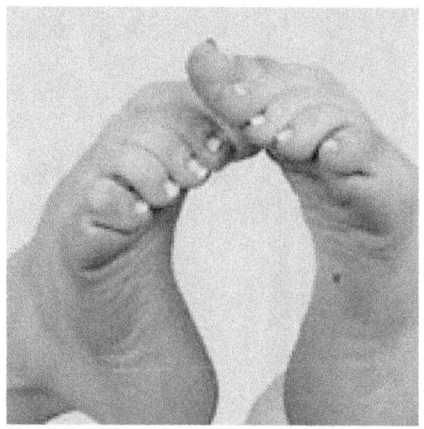

Arches of the feet replicating the World-vagina (outer view)

add your own foot mudra today

the most
outward moment
for the cosmos
is the newly born

the most
inward & acute
the newly deceased

the mushroom cloud of
Hiroshima: thus far, the
most radical threshold
experience composed
by the human species

the physical-etheric atmospheric "we"

The Poetics
of Warmth

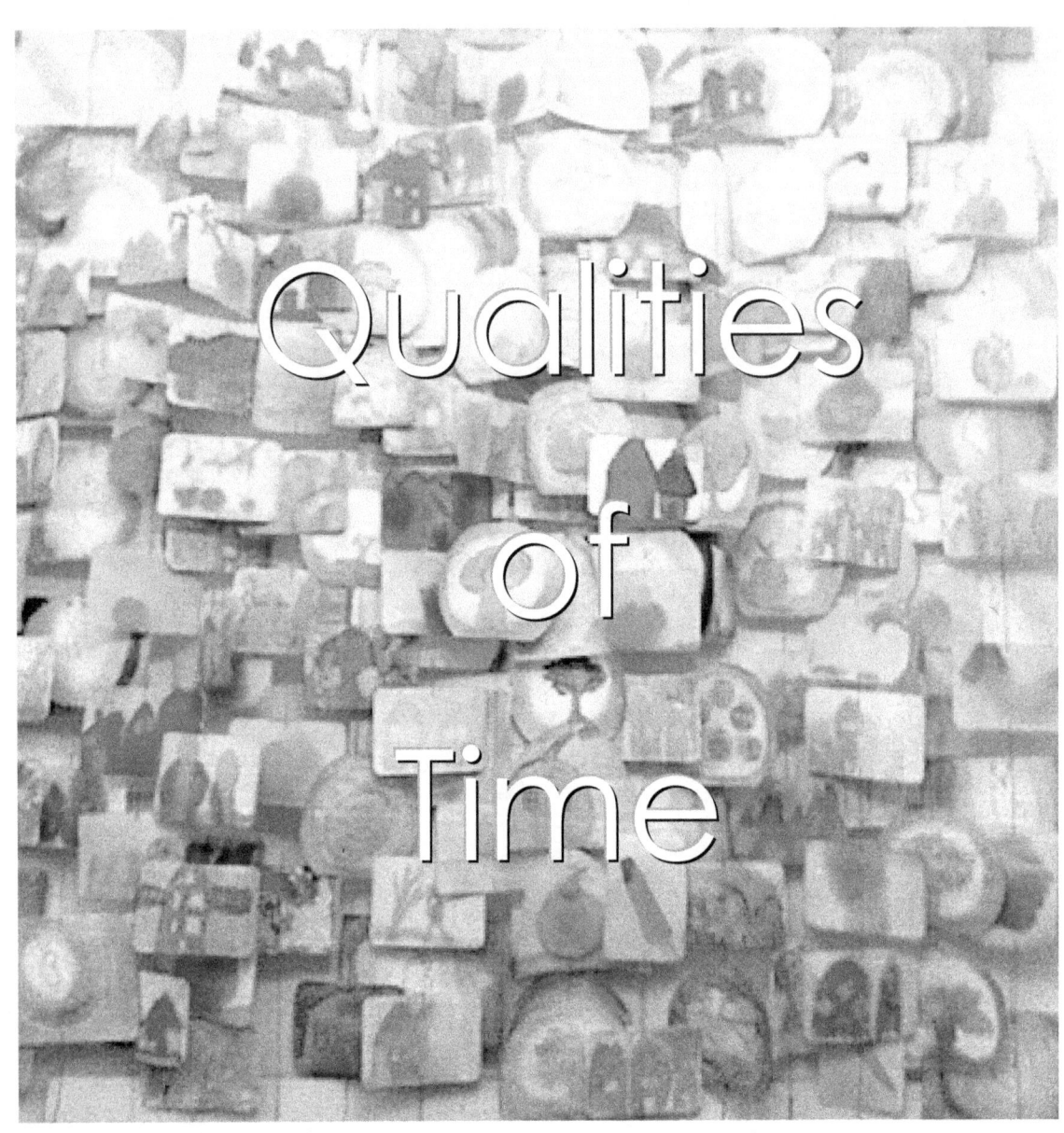

Qualities
of
Time

the senses
are gifts
surrendering
to reality

a tongue

don't

lie

the sky is
sometimes
an animal

right here
is the
entirety
of negative
space

the symbol for zero

inside the figure is a spell,

outside, physical existence

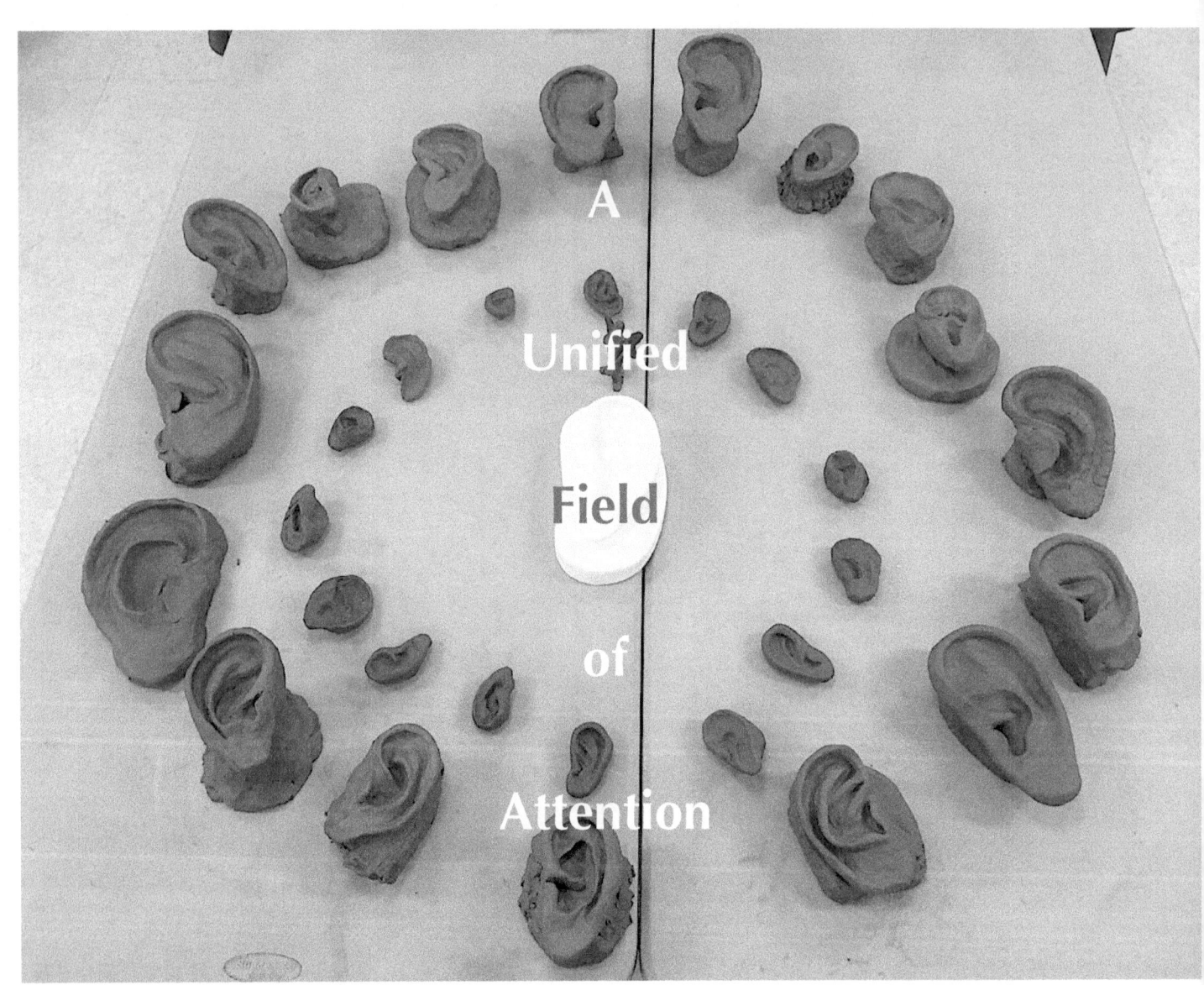

A

Unified

Field

of

Attention

the Unseen

harbors the

most

astonishing

of forms

the venerable edge
of the wonderfully
unpretentious

Theophanic Twin

....l am not afraid of anything. Not afraid of the dark. Not afraid of death. Not even Love. I am an atmosphere, a buried nova, a recovering arch, an undisturbed influorescence ready to live forever and die trying... giving all my breaths, tooth fillings, belongings and luminosity to the fire of wisdom. Into the flames, the glow, I rocket and am relieved. I am the whole of heaven's wish and now I'm yours because somehow you're a tenderness that reaches wide to show it, without the need to prove it.

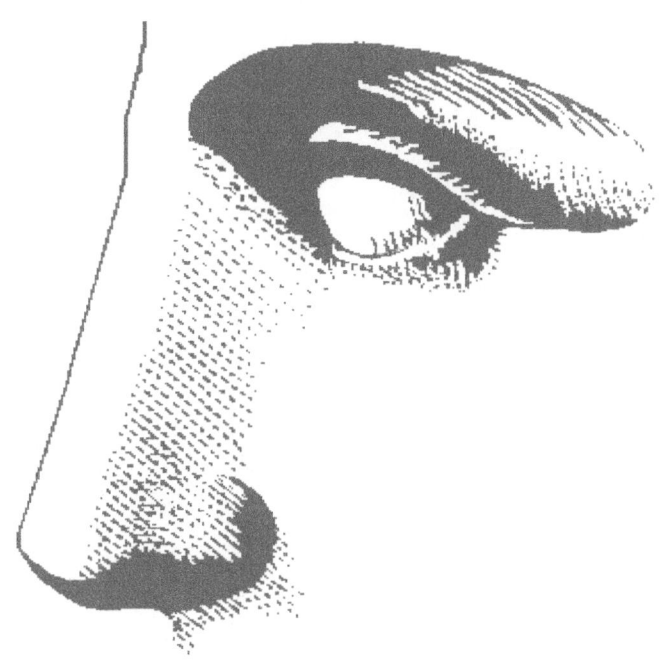

Fate tends
to put all its
eggs in
one basket

there's
more to the
I than
meets the *I*

there's
nowhere to hide
.
. .
so be everywhere
at once

this
is
destiny?

this is love
assembling

through porosity
lives limitless
devotion

Time has brought
us to a crucial
abyss,
a choice of self-
destruction or
creative
obliteration

evolve art: defy self-psychologizing

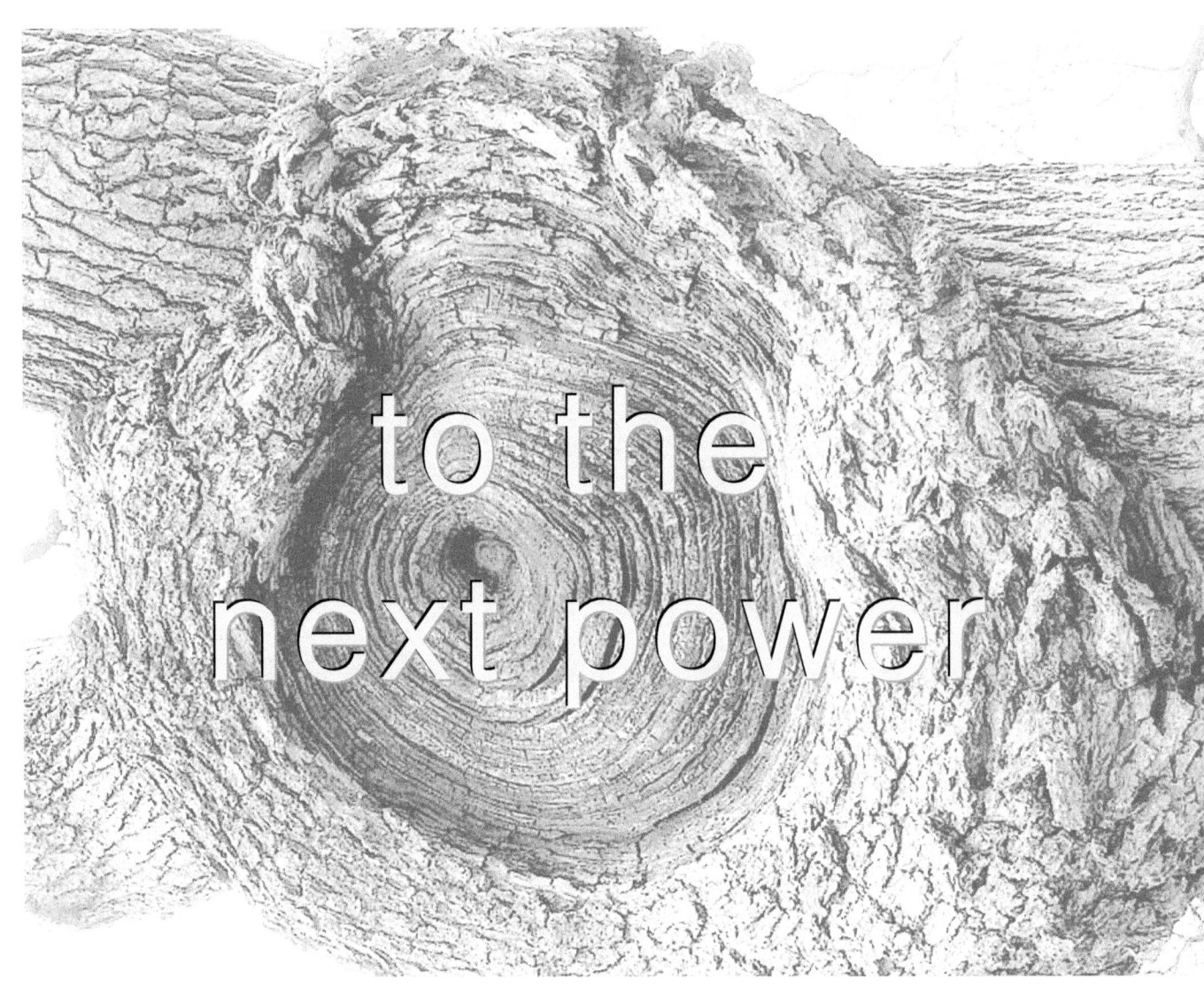

to the
next power

too much

puff

too little

pucker

touch moves
to devotion
on fire

transparence
is for anyone
planning to
re-incarnate

try your hand at the art of

reverse

sculpturing

a k i n   t o

unraveling a thorny

universe

unbinding desire

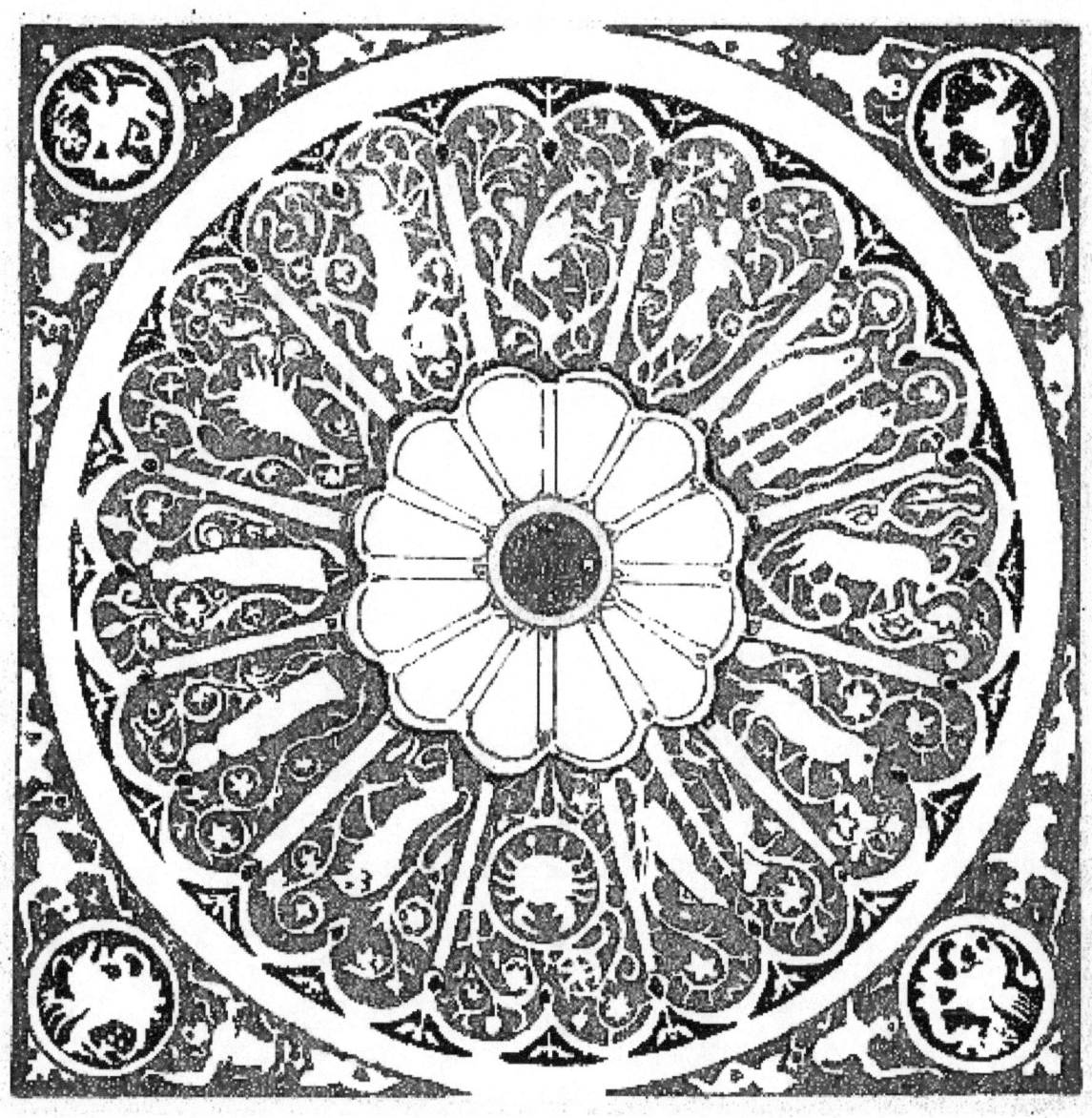

backwards

unbinding

the abyss

through

reverse

viewing

of the day

opened

unwrapping

the

mummification

wrought by

f e a r

up in the air,
sort of stars
below you

waking up

inside out

who are
becoming
the present

237

we are

the karma

of our

ancestors

they can see

you in your

v o i c e

we ourselves
create time;
it's not purely
something in
which we're
living

we pass
away
as we
abandon
our bones

241

just

one big

f ✲ cking

ray

of sunshine

nothing's
missing

(& we're not missing anything)

Biting Dust

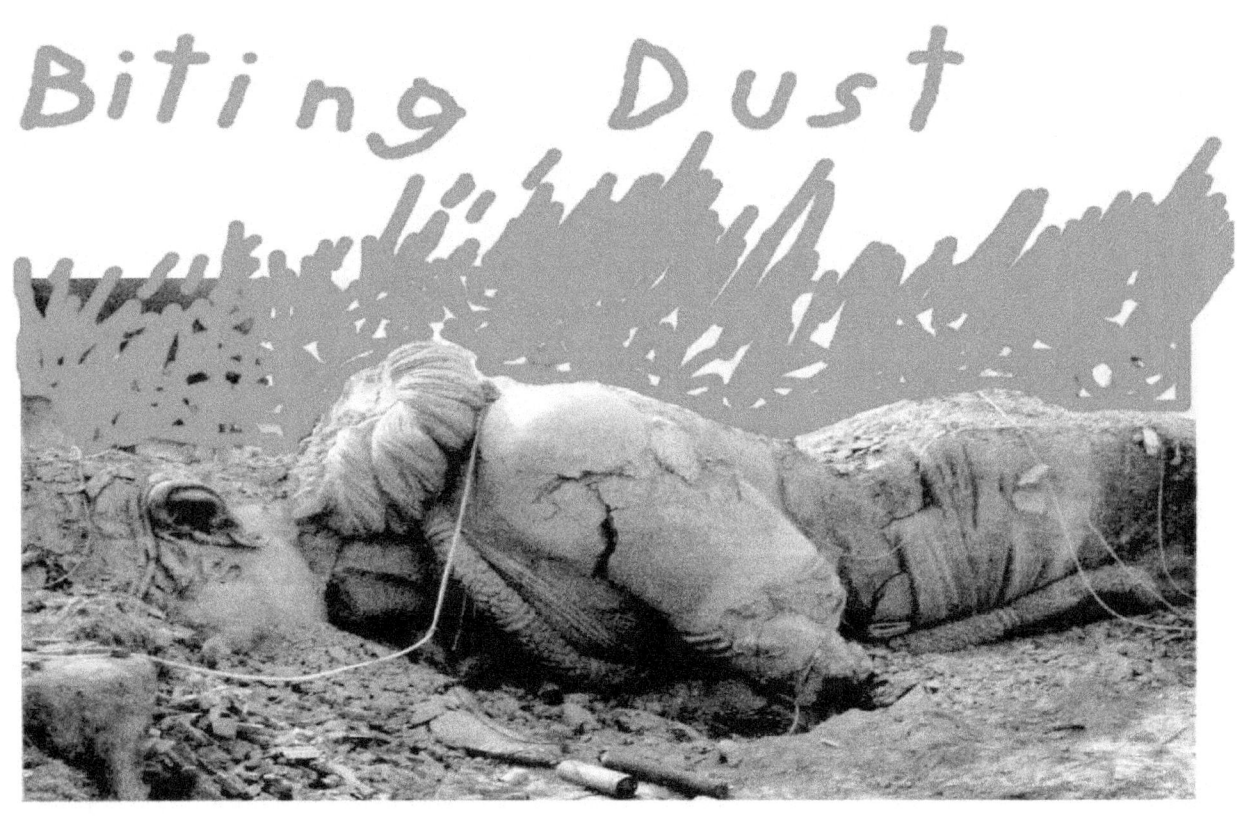

what can

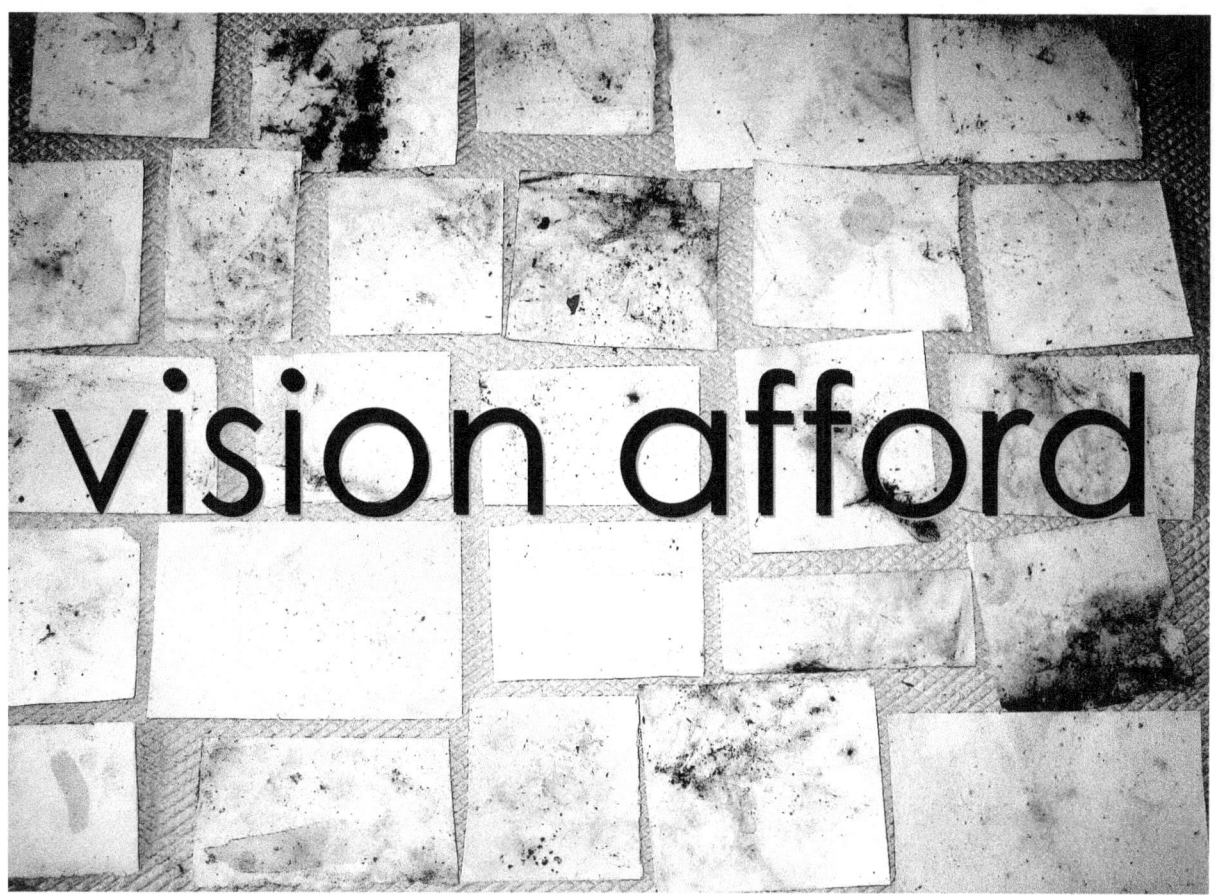

vision afford

to sacrifice?

what if

conversations

were guided

by the memory of

floating in the amnion?

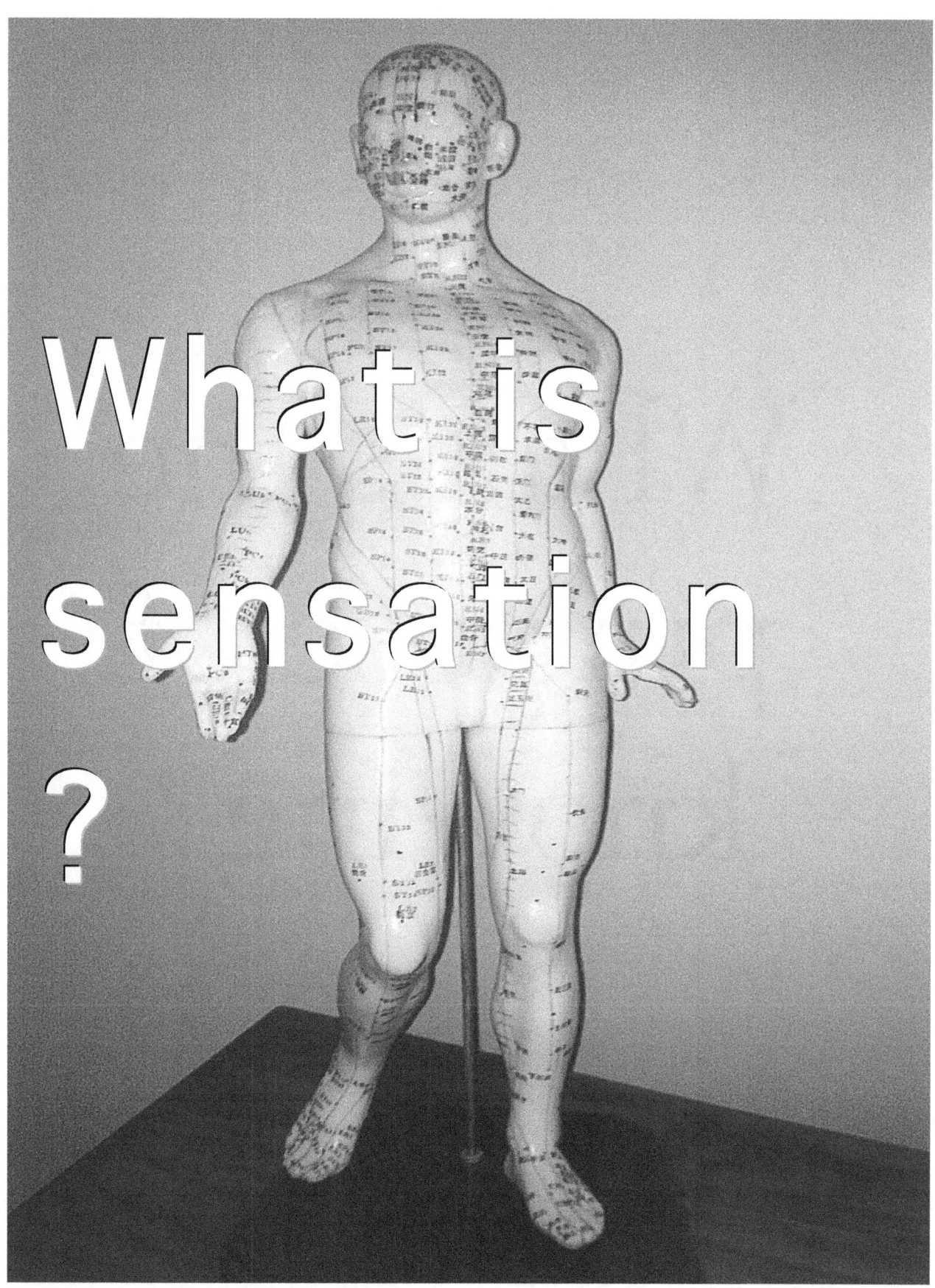

What is sensation?

What is the purpose of knowing?

What's creating this ocean of soul?

when

I'm

reborn

I

will...

how does art

free

matter

?

who mentioned
anything about
thwarting
the Illuminati ?

who'da thunk
that they
themselves
would love
purple?

nearly

everything

sounds

like

advertising

why

is

this

all

so

necessary?

why look
when you
can see?

Why make art?

To find a way *into* something?

To enable others to see *what* you feel?

Why make art?

Will

with smell
experience starts
with vulnerability,
not permission

without intimacy there
wouldn't be something
called the future

excretion

sets up

time

&

space

origins live within questions

questions within origins

the prospect of togetherness

lives through

X + Y

you & me:
worth the
effects

you are
an original
catalyst
for disarming
the small-
hearted

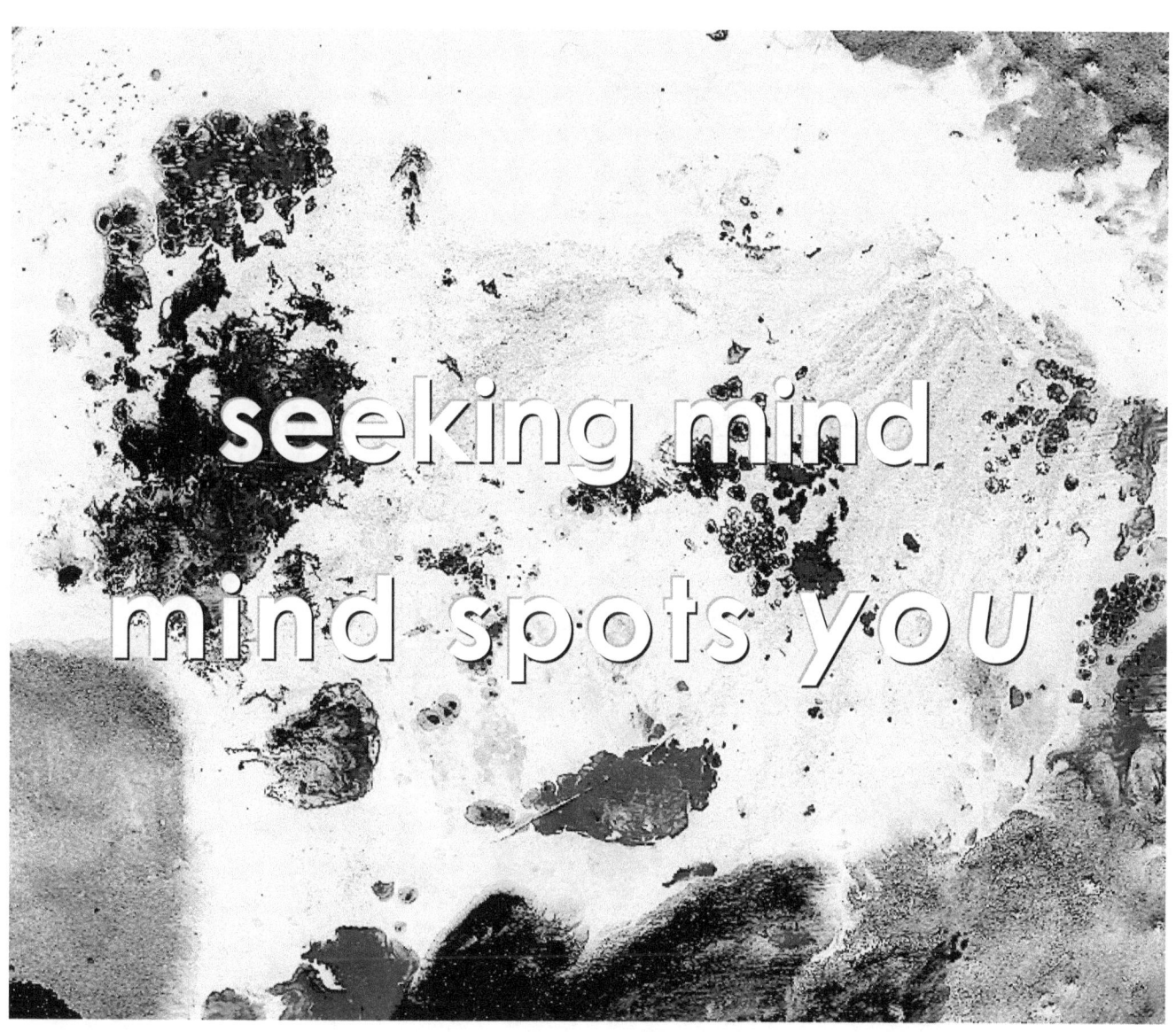

some find it necessary to be "in a state"

—directly overcome by mood

or temperament—

in order to feel existence

you don't really
experience
sensation
until your soul is
touched tip to toe

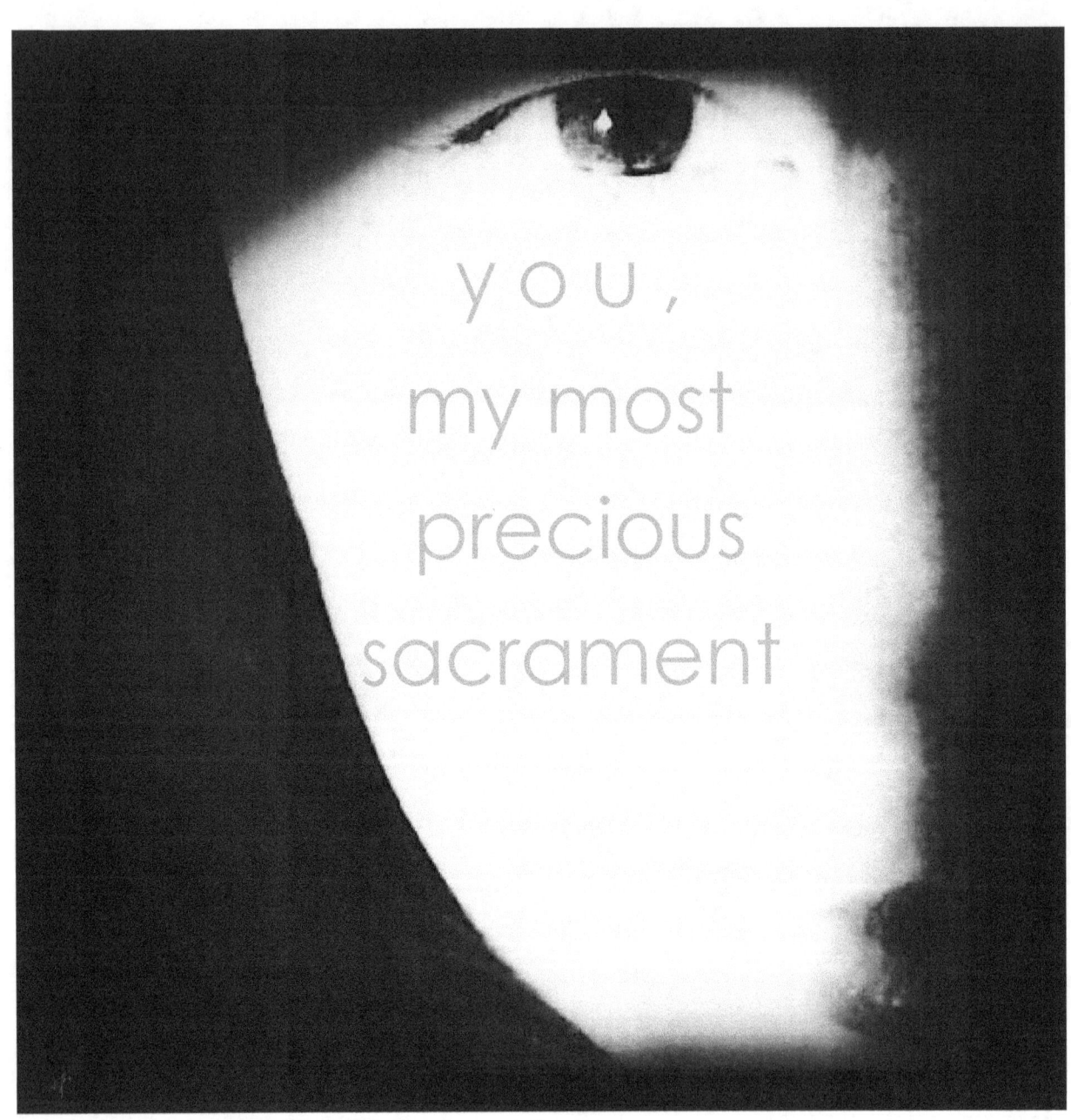

if you wanna
be a dream,
dream
in a primeval-
futurist
kind of way

you're

with

↑
← ↕ →
↓

your aura **can** have the smell of freshly mowed grass

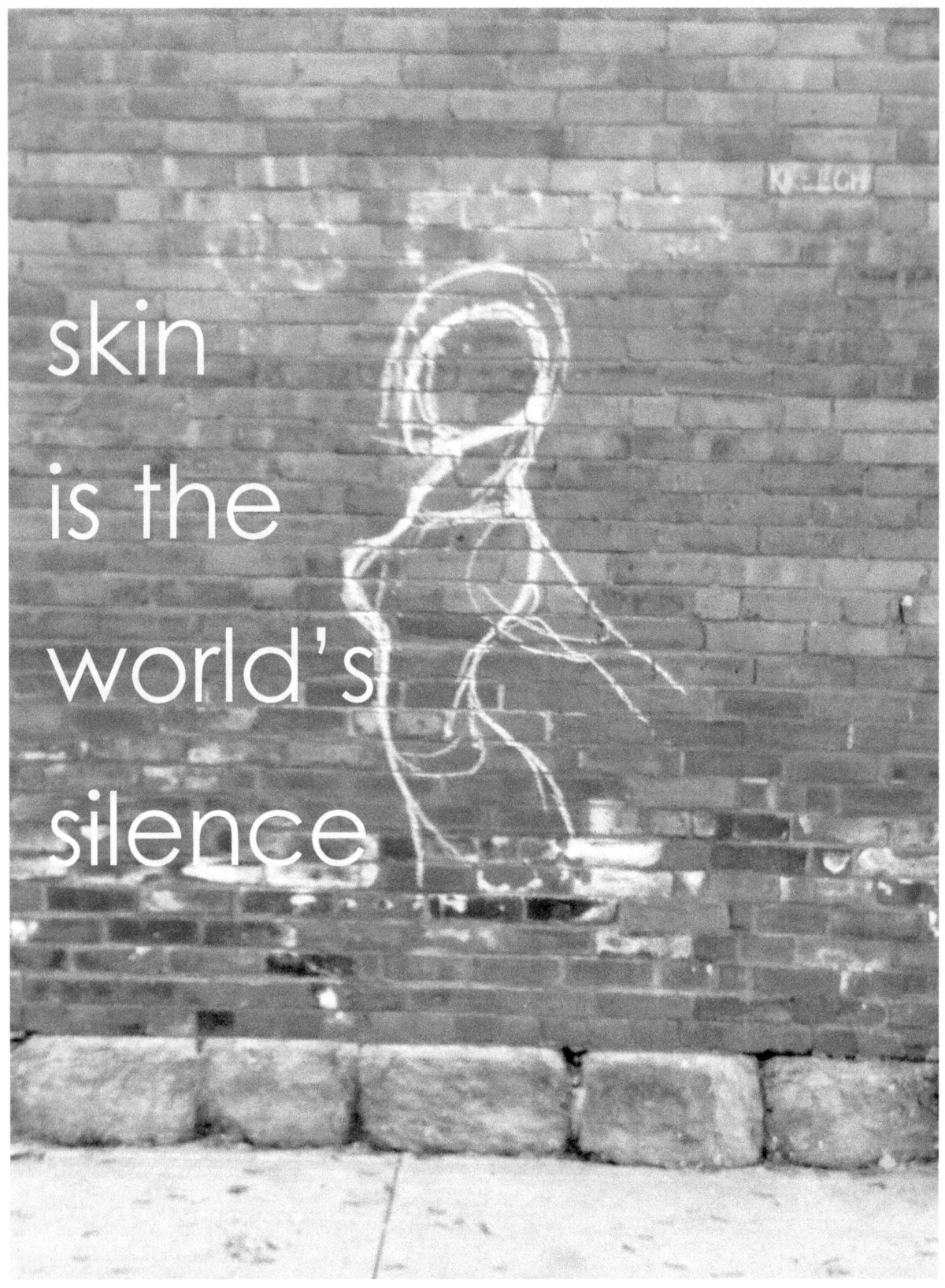

an enduring
instance of
silent music,
begins,
then ends

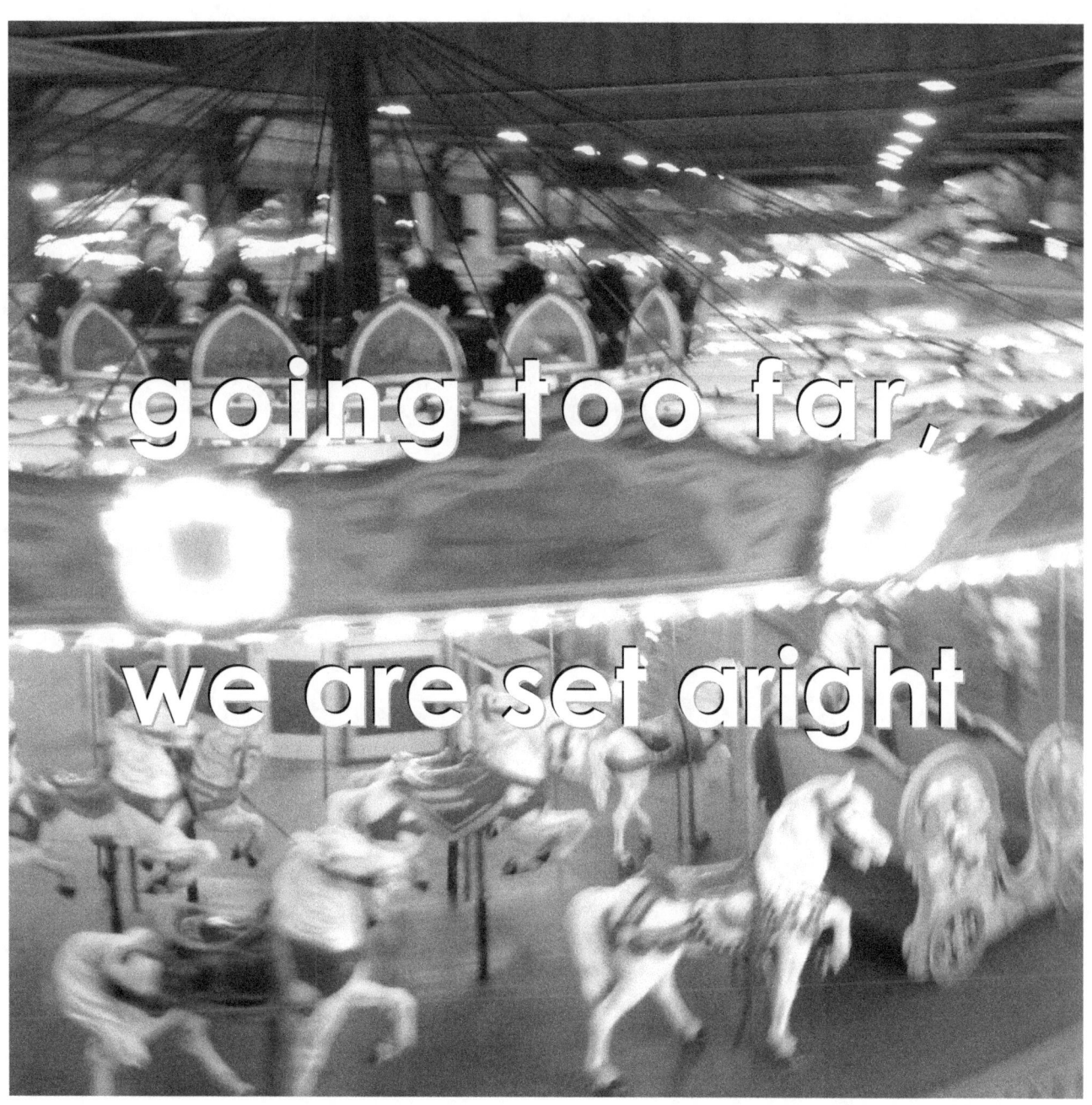

there

are no

physical

causes

please do
not protect
me from my
ignorance

Culture With Benefits

rub a little mother's milk gently on the surface of notable statues

recite the Divine Comedy behind an immense wall

lovingly apply birdseed to your feet

hurl paintings directly upwards into the air

lightly brush your nose on a distinguished work of art

touch Saturn with your left hand, the Sun with your right

invent something while standing upside down

Aura Spotting

this moment
is the gesture
of every
effect

touch

enlightenment

with your body

slurped

back

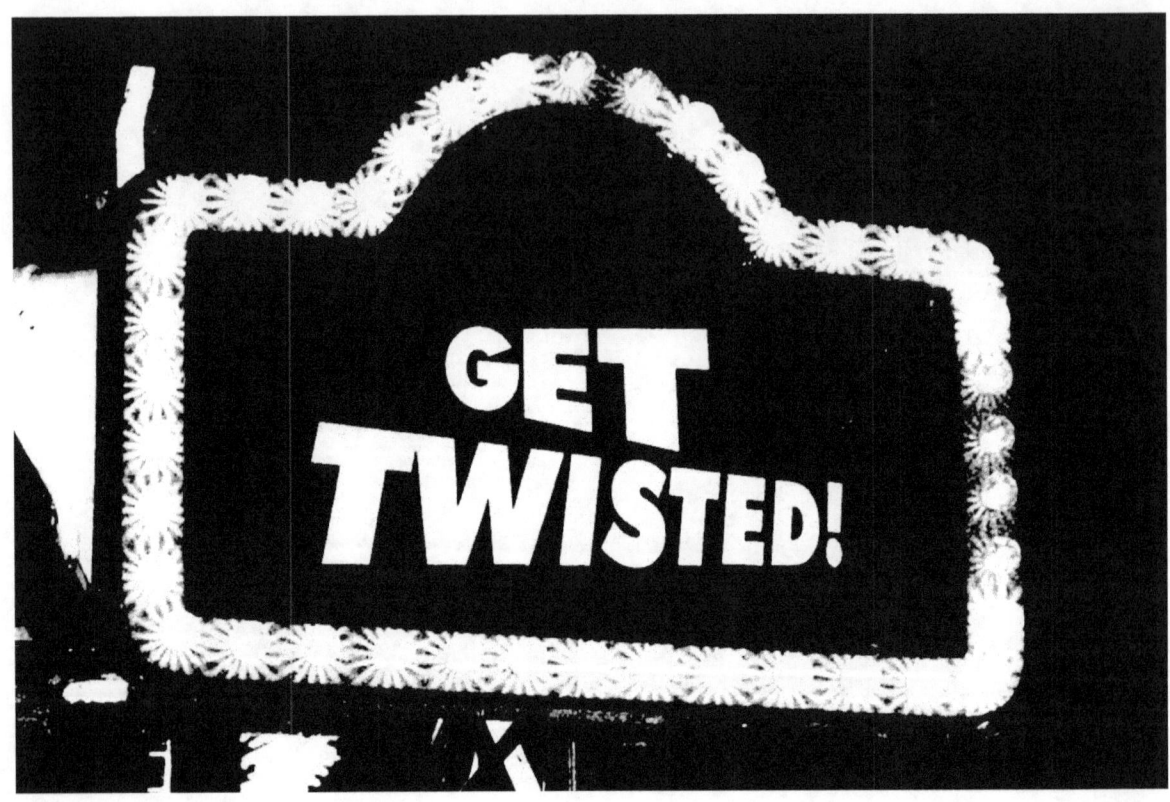

into

emptiness

education is
obliged to guide
the public
to discern bullshit
as if it were an ad
on a billboard

egotism &
& self-ruin

beginnings

everywhere

ERASING CULTURAL NOSTALGIA

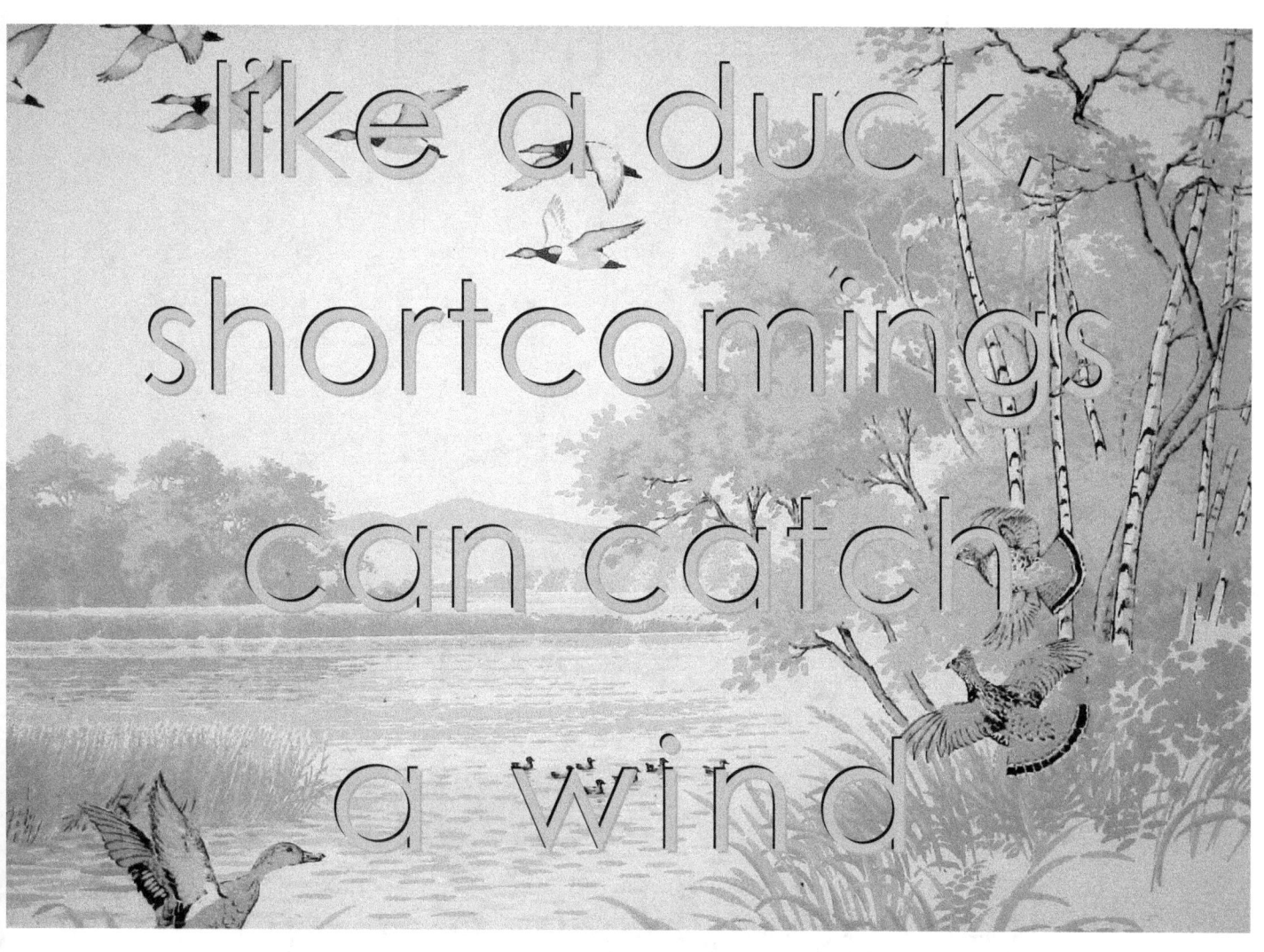

everybody

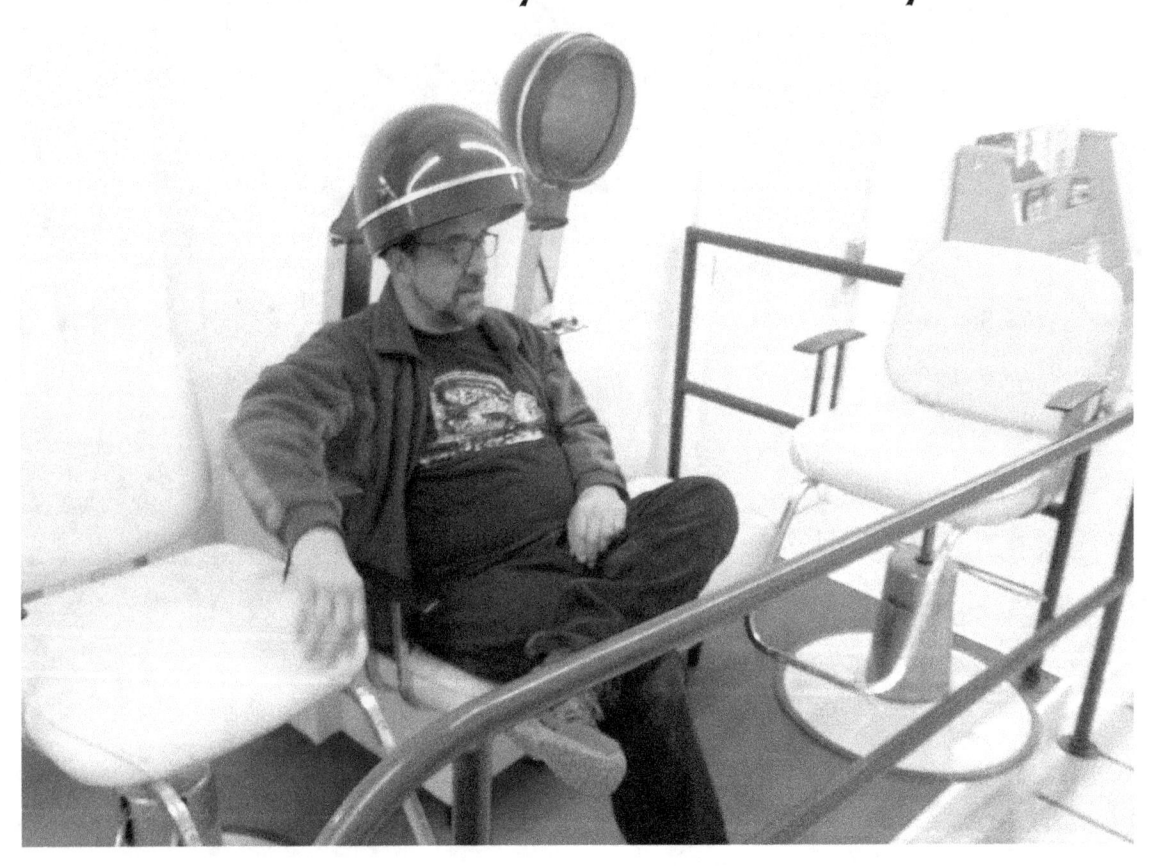

sets everybody else up

is the mineral
world the "end"
of desiring?

our

karma

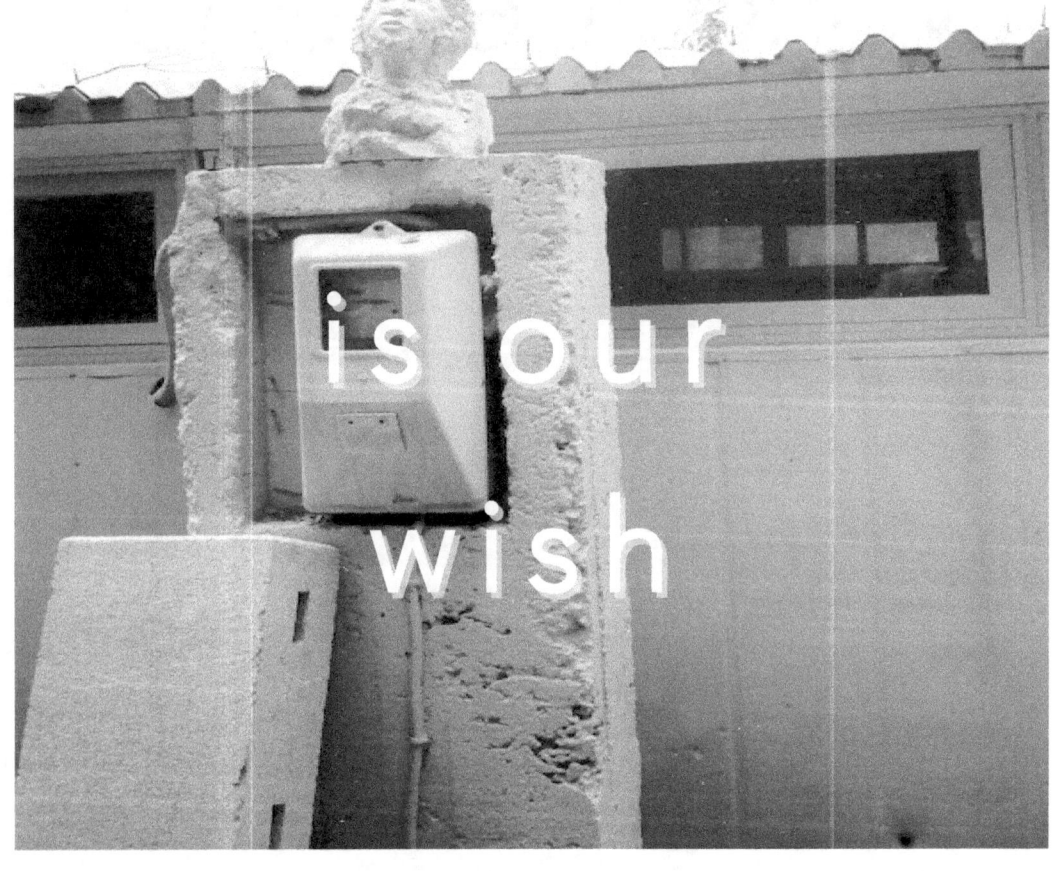

is our

wish

it's all precious
since
it's all blood

employing
electricity became
the significant event
for wrapping up
the Kali Yuga

ruins

turn out to be

limitless

changing
the horizon of
inter-egoity
doesn't empty the
self's effort

the
avant-garde-
inclined
bourgeoisie
arrange for the
maximum
comfort zone

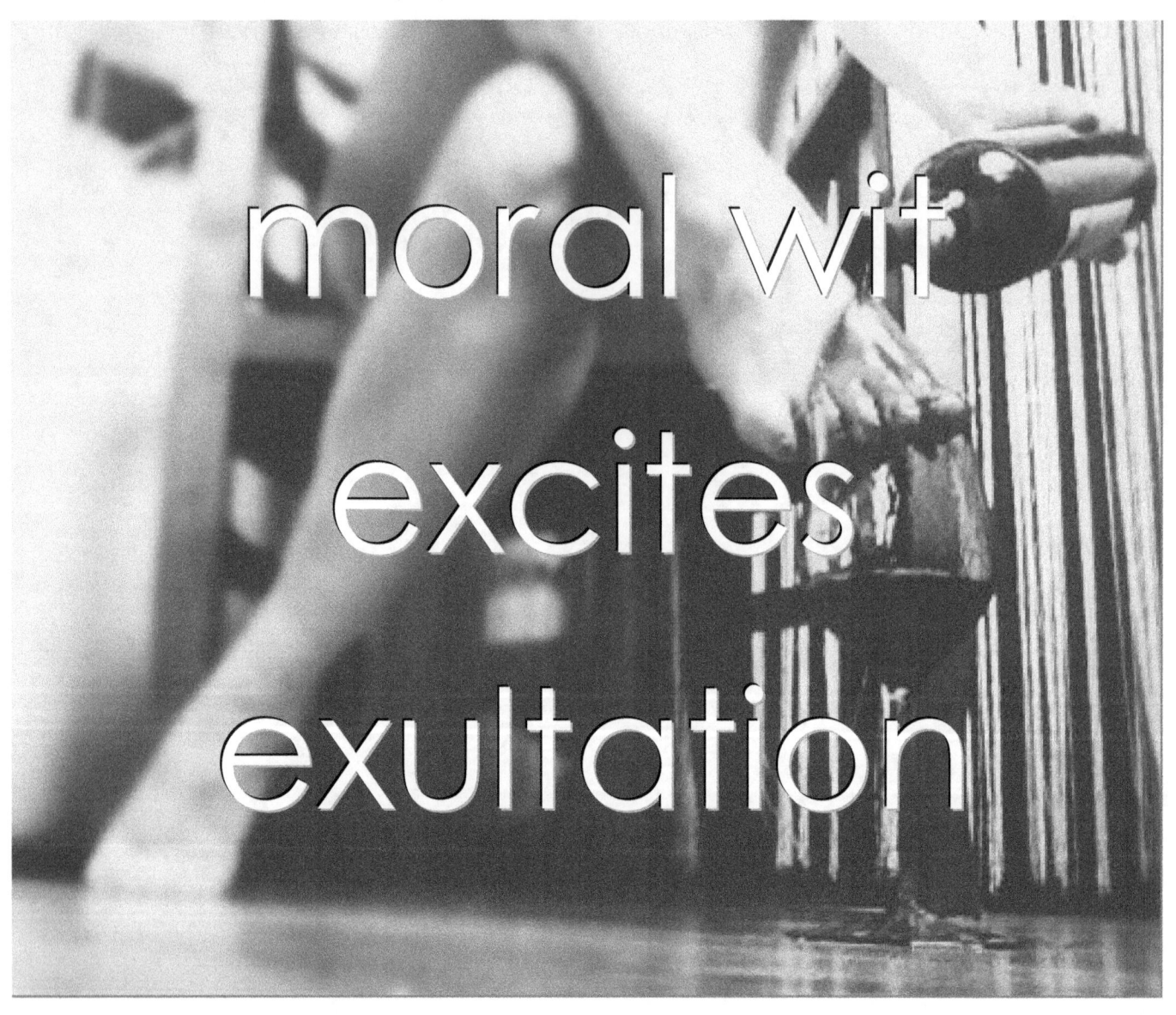

moral wit
excites
exultation

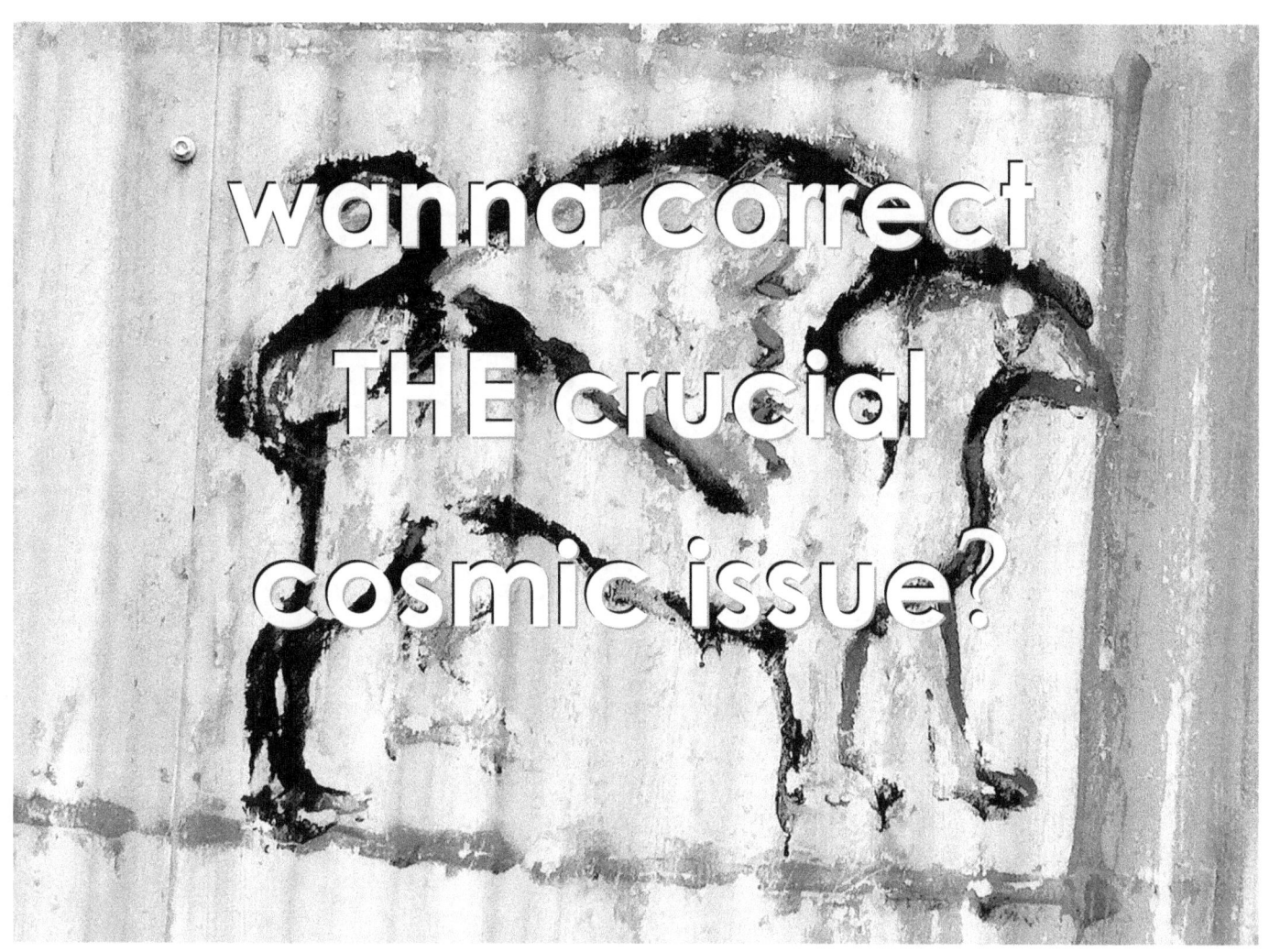

wanna correct
THE crucial
cosmic issue?

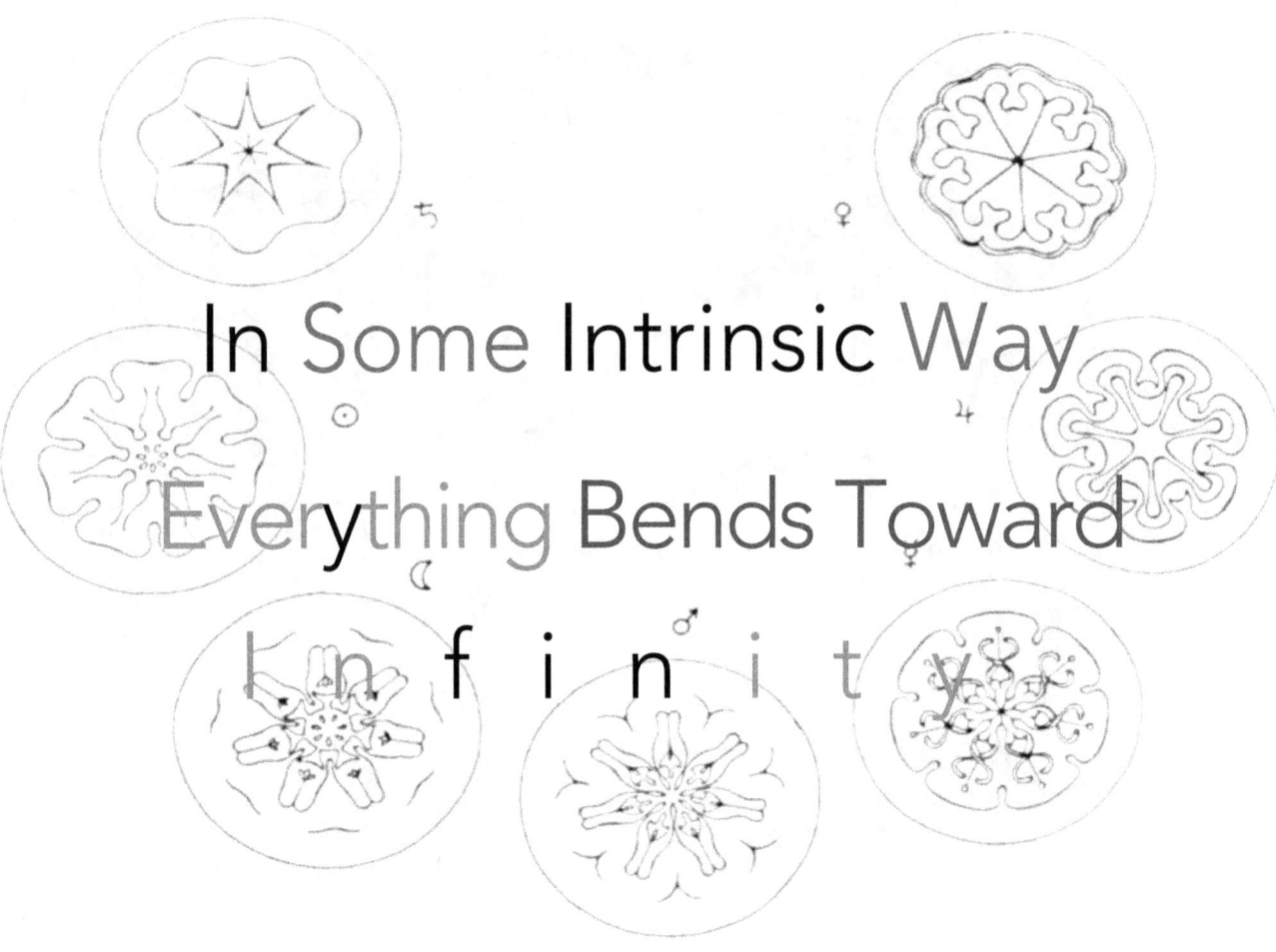

In Some Intrinsic Way

Everything Bends Toward

I n f i n i t y

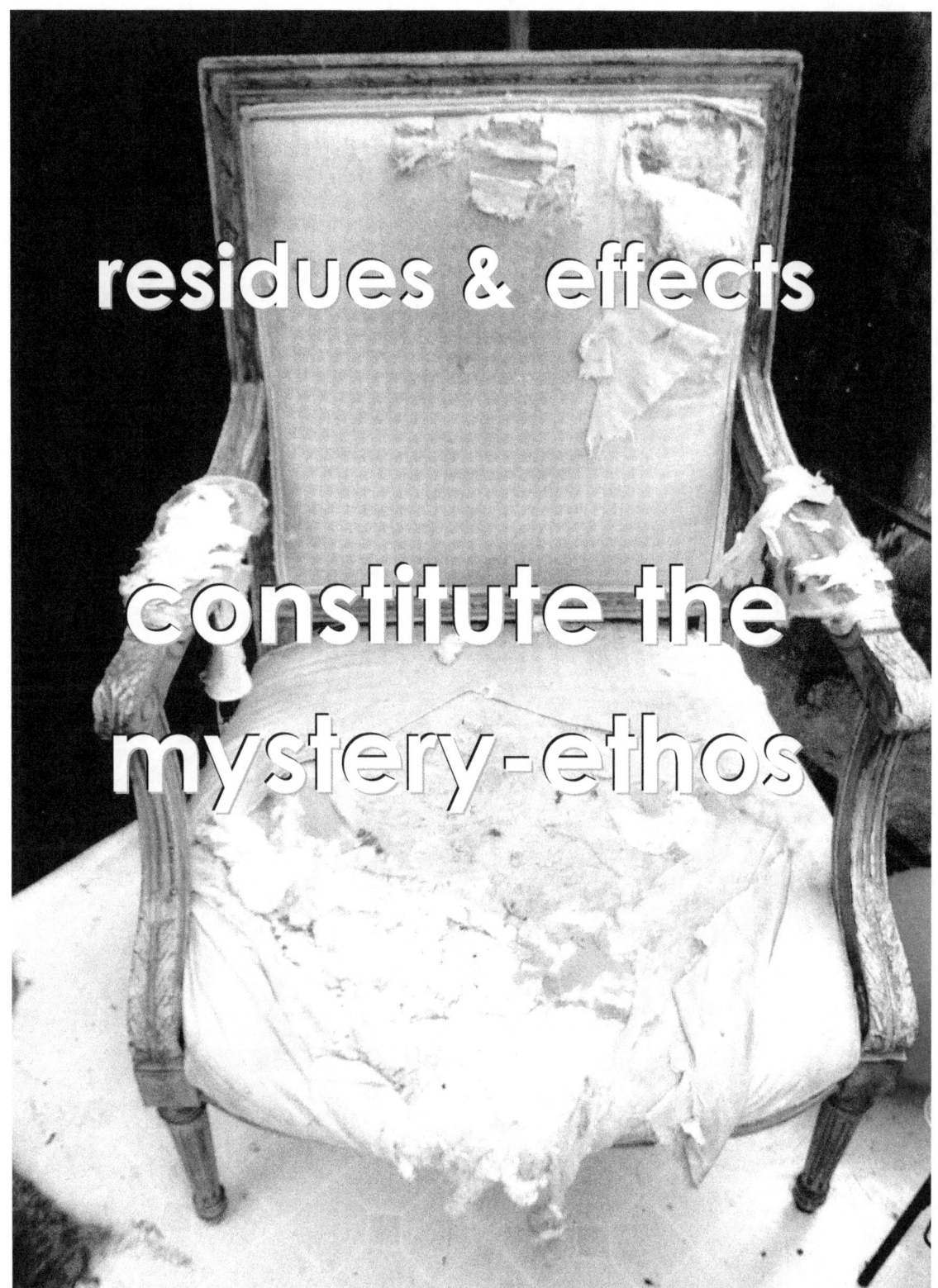

residues & effects

constitute the

mystery-ethos

299

the slightest bit of bone

carries spiritual weight

ready to be drunk back into the galaxy's Imagination?

Grace

is a spore

in need of expansion

everyone

looks

younger

in

pajamas

everything

is turning...

everything

everything

EVERYTHING

the heart is the
organ of evolution

evolution arises
inside out the
heart

experiencing
observation
is like
disappearing

reflect matter in form

extreme function

form in matter

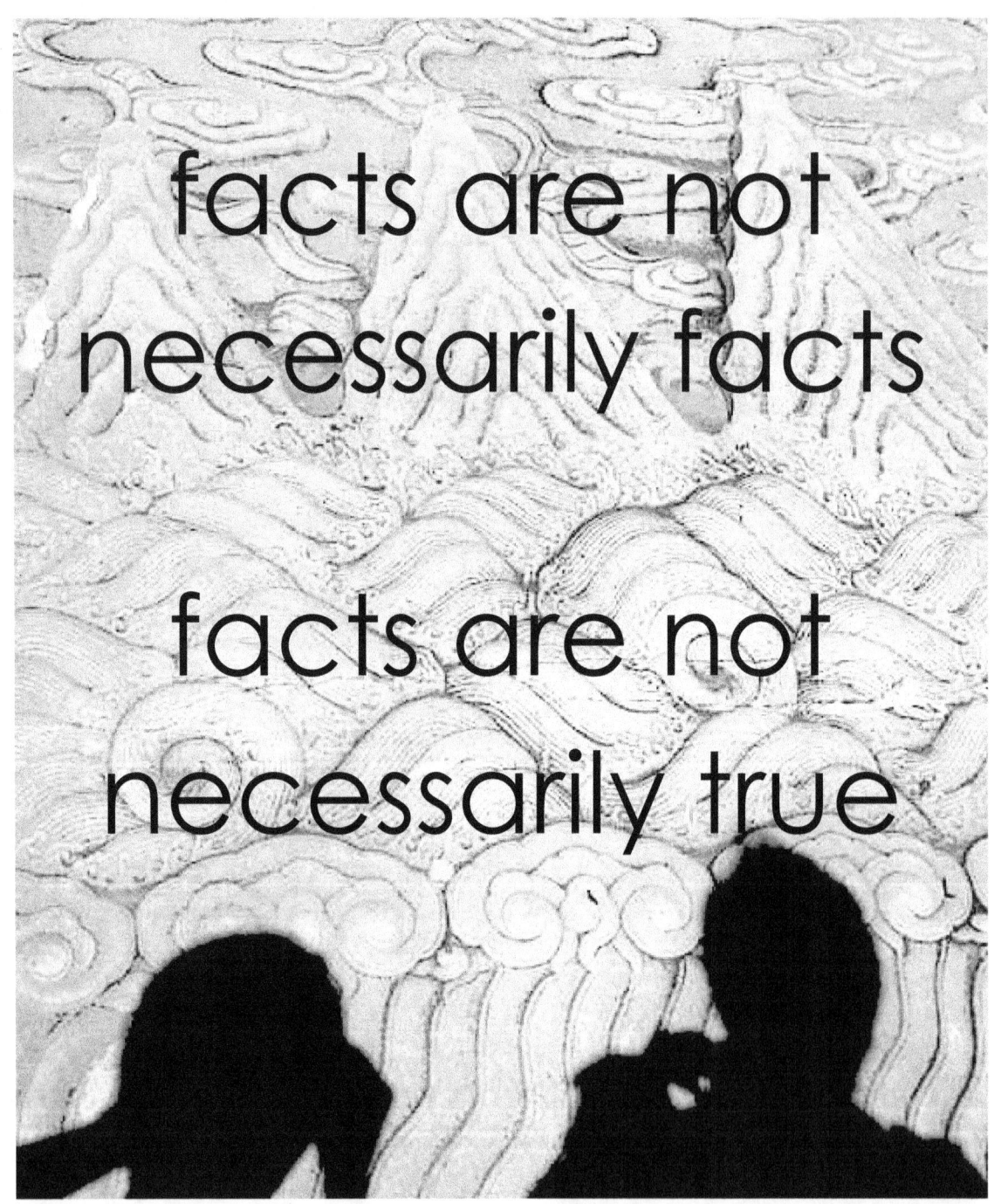

facts are not
necessarily facts

facts are not
necessarily true

7, 🌍00, 🌏00, 🌎00

of us

need to

make it work

Andrew Franck's writings include

The Transparent Bride, The Art of Porosity, Mantras and Musical Solutions,

Exercises In Romantic Understanding, Stillness In Motion and The Holy Bodies Circuit